PUSH FORWARD

Tira Avanti

PUSH FORWARD

Written by I.R. Thornton
Co-Author Joey Tomaselli

ARCHWAY
PUBLISHING

Archway Publishing books may be ordered through booksellers or by contacting:

Archway Publishing
1663 Liberty Drive
Bloomington, IN 47403
www.archwaypublishing.com
844-669-3957

Author photo by Justin Morris.
Front cover image by Julia Talbot.

ISBN: 978-1-6657-0491-5 (sc)
ISBN: 978-1-6657-0490-8 (hc)
ISBN: 978-1-6657-0492-2 (e)

Library of Congress Control Number: 2021906091

Print information available on the last page.

Archway Publishing rev. date: 4/9/2021

PART ONE

Prologue

He could hear the old guy working out in the garden. The astonishing smell of cut grass passed him on small rafts, intruders through the open doors and windows. The remarkable tang from the lawn was sweeter than ever before; a concentrated beauty like the sheer whiteness of blossom described by palliative cancer patients fading in the spring. There was a good reason his senses were on alert, and this shall soon be explained. The gardener had liberated this aroma as he struck down thousands of blades of young grass. In their prime. He grafted out there in his spare time, powered by a source of energy that compelled him to work, made him happiest when he was working, and pushed on by a desire to keep working so he was able to make things as beautiful for his family as he possibly could.

"I could never work as hard as my father did for us but if only, IF ONLY, he knew how hard I had worked not to give up. To not end it all. To not kill myself," Joey thought.

People like to say there is nothing like a funeral to concentrate the mind. Even more so, if it is *your* own funeral and you know there are just minutes, perhaps an hour or two, left. Once the decision is made, there is apparently sometimes a strange freedom from the agony. But not with Joey. Joey Tomaselli - kind, handsome, funny, and tender Joey Tomaselli - hurt more than ever.

Bleach. Poison. Rope. He did not fancy cutting himself.

He was like a wounded animal, curled up at the end of the sofa on that broiling August Saturday. Like some poor critter one might see on a National Geographic documentary, already in the boa constrictor's grip. Done deal. Just a startled but doped look in the eye.

He had just had his third shower of the day, and he was more worried about contaminating the material on the couch than any human should have been.

The hedge trimmer started, and more of nature's finery was about to perish at the generous gardener's hand. It didn't need to die. What a waste. The strewn lawn trimmings were already browning in the heat. A single maple leaf was caught in a rare breeze and decided unilaterally to join the grave of clippings below. Three more followed in sympathy within a minute.

The young man's friends were all away, at cottages, out of the city, with girls, drinking, laughing, swimming and making love. Then laughing and making love some more. He could only guess. His island of solitude was his alone. It had been this way for a while.

He could hear his mother in the kitchen. His loneliness was all-encompassing and not because of the lack of love of this woman and the fine, proud man currently taming nature on his property. His lonesomeness was there in spite of their adoration and loyalty and utter worship for their own flesh and blood. Her red hair, white skin and emerald eyes were the proud Italian *tricolore* that flew over that corner of Canada. The independent state of Silvio and Mary sat on that rich and fertile quadrant of Ontario. The children had wanted for nothing there. It was their land. They had made it their own, and they were benevolent rulers. And now the old man tended his patch of turf as his forefathers had the pastures of that Italian hillock, proud and meticulous. He knew how he wanted it and how it should look, just as the car engines he fine-tuned and fixed over the years, in melting summers and unreasonably vicious winters. All for the citizens of that single address in Brampton. His Mary, the two girls and Joey.

But no one is perfect. And for every engine he sorted out and every buttercup or tulip that thrived and wilted within his boundaries, it was perhaps just a moment that he did not therefore have on his hands to tell his son that he loved him. But Joey knew this, for he had also seen his own personal National Geographic documentary on that fine species, the Italian male.

So, this was all the more astonishing when Silvio marched in that day, sweat on his brow, and came to his only son, lowered himself to his haunches and to eye level with his boy. He fixed his gaze upon him as if he sensed to perfection what was required.

His hand touched Joey, and he spoke.

"Come on, buddy."

And in the remaining few seconds before the magic wore off, the old mechanic fixed everything in the world of his only boy. The boy then knew his suicidal actions would only hurt beyond comprehension this small nation state of Silvio and Mary the most. And the Italians are nothing if not patriotic.

"I don't like seeing you like this," he said.

And he paused, stood, and went back to tending his western border. It was the act of a true leader.

Chapter 1

We know all of what happened to Joey Tomaselli – that remarkable and tragic tale - because that poor boy left us a generous record of it. It was recorded for posterity. And from that it is now committed to paper. Black and white. And you now hold in it your hand. This is what he endured before he reached the end. Even in his abject state, he wanted to help others. It was just the way he was brought up. A kind and thoughtful boy. Would never hurt a fly. Would make his *nonna* so proud.

It was the eighties. The television was a boxy, heavy old thing. The picture seemed barely contained by the ungainly and rectangular edges, and its flashing images reached out from their small prison. Yet this was the generous old girl that had delivered the beauty and the thrill, the ecstasy and the euphoria of the 1982 World Cup in Spain. Italy won and became World Champions. Long before the crescendo of frenzy and bliss, angry and frustrated male gestures and violet invective had been hurled in the direction of the screen in those early and tawdry games. By a freak of the system, the *Azzurri* sneaked through the first stage without winning a game, and barely mustered a shot on target, but then faced with the might of Argentina and Brazil in the next stage flourished, prodded and provoked into doing so by necessity. The caterpillar that had spun itself a silky cocoon to avoid the media poison from the Roman homeland, transformed into the chrysalis and emerged as the resplendent butterfly under the scorching Iberian sun. The names of the three goal-scorers that helped Italy lift the trophy, "Rossi, Tardelli, Altobelli" are still sung with the gusto of a Pavarotti opera across stadia to this day. Whenever Silvio looked at that television after that night, he would recall the rapture. His son, Joey was only two at the time, and therefore the contraption in the corner would form different memories for him.

Perhaps thirty people were again crammed into that basement, which to the six-year-old Joey, in the spirit of the grown man re-visiting his primary school and realising how ridiculously small the rooms are, looked pretty big.

There were Ferrari posters on the subterranean walls. Silvio had put them up, and then had added some of that gloried soccer team in blue that defined a year. Silvio's homemade wine, bottled each September with an engineer's precision and pride, completed the Holy Trinity. The altar was the buzzing and flashing screen.

There was a buffet table against a wall, with a casino-sized spread. Plates of veggies, meats, and different kinds of pasta almost filled the table, proudly presented by the matriarch, Mary. On the corners of the table stood adequate provisions of his *vino* to give a warm buzz to the Nazarene and all twelve disciples. There were ashtrays, with smoke perpetually coiling towards the yellowy ceiling.

Most of the men huddled there, arguing over cars, while the fragrant and coiffured ladies relished their time together, their tones lowered. They could all speak together and yet still not a word was missed.

He couldn't care less. His gaze was fixed to the screen in front of him. He was hypnotized, unable to move. The images on the screen were just too terrifyingly captivating for him to do so.

Every so often one of the adults would go behind the bar next to the TV and grab a glass of cognac, but still Joey's eyes stayed set on the screen. He was transfixed at the images dancing across it, and his hands were clinging to a soft pillow on his lap.

The year was 1986. Chernobyl had exploded. Freddie Mercury was still alive, vacuuming in a dress. *Star Wars* was popular, and Oprah was settling on her throne. Television ruled, and her subjects sat in obeisance, all in deferential respect to the low-ish budget story called *Swamp Thing*, a Wes Craven film of a DC Comic.

And it is important to him, because it is about to frighten the young boy, and plant a seed of terror.

It might be a seed that sets in motion an avalanche of fear that would impact his whole life.

The little boy didn't laugh with the rest of them.

He figured he was the only one not enjoying the movie, but he couldn't say that. Not in an Italian home. That wasn't the motto there. His only choice was to remain silent, seemingly rooted to his spot on the carpet.

A sense of anxiety crept up then from inside his stomach, rising to the surface, just as a sudden cacophony of music erupted from the screen and a monster's ghoulish hand grabbed a victim.

The film sparked a pair of recent traumatic memories. It was as if his mind was now protecting him from the immediate terror in the movie by reminding him of other past horrors. He tried to think of more pleasant things, but it was useless.

First, he remembered his previous birthday. He had been in his front yard by Silvio's polished sports cars. It was a large family event

Italian-style. Kids ran wild and free in the front garden, and the men drank wine and smoked cigarettes to ease their way through the party. He was the centre of attention.

His neighbors had a German shepherd called Gino, a bored and mean beast. Every day, the twisted, tormented and single-minded hound would trot and canter along the fence that divided the two houses. In any kind of weather, the crazed mutt seemed to have one single duty; to terrorize him and his two older sisters, Sandra and Nadia. Gino's mad eyes and his vicious bark appeared to be never far away. He patrolled the barrier with the vigilance of an ambitious soldier, sensing that one day he would breach the border, and find his prey. Like the obsidian terrorist, he *only* had to get through once.

He was on his tricycle enjoying his birthday, sipping on his favorite apple juice. This was the day that Gino escaped. All those days of frustration meant that the liberated monster would take him down as his first target. The moment he sensed the beast was out of his pen, he leaped off his small vehicle, believing he could outrun the creature. Gino caught him with ease, bringing him down with a meaty paw on the small lad's back. It was that National Geographic documentary again; a seasoned lion on a helpless young antelope. The prey's face smashed onto the concrete, bringing scarlet to the boy's beak. Tears diluted the crimson, and his mother, almost as swift to reach Joey as the canine, picked him up from the ground. Silvio watched.

Gino was caught and dragged back to his enclosure. This was all he had wanted. He'd gladly spend the rest of his days there now, content in his fuzzy memory of the day he fulfilled his earthly mission. He had now left his pawprint on the planet, and this was a bruise, a mental scarring on a young boy's mind. He would never trust dogs again. He would avoid them like any sane person would do with syphilis. Or parking tickets.

A battered birthday boy blew out the candles on his Bert and Ernie cake, as his loving grandmother held him and smiled. Then he wouldn't let anyone cut the cake or eat it, because he loved Bert and

Ernie far too much, the tender and bloodied child, disproving the theory that dogs are fine judges of character.

Back in the basement in front of *Swamp Thing*, there was an ad break on the television. To his left and right, everyone gasped or laughed with excitement. He tried turning his head away, but his spine seemed to be trapped, unable to move freely. He felt helpless. Each scene cranked up the horror. This was not a terror that made him concerned for the characters in the plot. This was a direct attack on *his* soul.

In a trick of perhaps perverse self-preservation, his mind wandered again. To the second of his pair of bad memories. Why could he not think of something comforting?

This time, he was reminded of that past summer at his parents' cottages and the hotel in Wasaga Beach. They owned and rented out these holiday homes, while keeping one free for their family to use.

The beach was crowded in the summers. The exodus of the city had started the weekend school was out. A mass of humanity had moved. Each kid had their own vision of how they would spend the summer. Some children went swimming, others played tag. He collected beer bottles with his ten-year-old friend, Gianni, so they could make money to play the arcade games. Gianni's dad was Silvio's business partner. His family also had a cottage of their own. Because his pal was older, it was like hanging around with a teenager. His friend was larger than life, and naturally, seemed to have all the answers and knew what to do.

The two boys used to take a trash bag and go door-to-door collecting Budweiser and Labatt Blue bottles from the cottages. It was an easy and quick buck. They met all kinds of people, as one would do going door-to-door. Some people smiled, others frowned, and some just shrugged and said, 'Sure.'

There was one occasion that now haunted him His friend and he approached a cottage where a couple of college kids were staying with their girlfriends. As a joke, one of the older boys told him to take the bottle from in-between one of the girls' thighs. Their giggles were hardly concealed. He didn't mind though. He was the type of boy to take his shirt off as soon as he saw a girl at the beach, flexing what muscles he had and striking a pose as they passed. He remembered that any time a girl, of any age, looked at him, he would take his hidden comb or sometimes just his hand, and run it over his head slowly like some latter-day Danny Zuko. Smooth.

And so, he took the bottle from the tan thighs of some eager Samantha or Cathy and went on his way, happy for the opportunity to brush against a girl's skin that his instinct told him was sensitive and forbidden, *and* the chance to make some a few cents.

Then things turned sour. Even his fonder memories were being vanquished in front of that swamp film.

That summer day, Gianni had left to go back to his cottage for a snack, while he and his sister, Nadia decided to go to the beach. Soon he needed the bathroom to defecate. He told his sister.

He finally found a public washroom. It stank.

With little choice, young Joey, with his trash bag of bottles left outside against the stone wall of the little white building, went in.

While sitting on the rank toilet, two teenage boys barrelled in, telling jokes and laughing loudly, their obnoxiousness as potent as the stench from the stalls. Hearing his straining, passing of gas and echo against the bowl, the two pushed at the loose piece of wood with a faulty bolt-lock, and burst into laughter as the poor kid, his shorts around his ankles, tried to cover himself up. They stood cackling, pointing crooked fingers at him as he sat, exposed and shamed. The shaft of light from the summer sun shone through the open entrance-way, and down upon his bony knees. He had his arm outstretched towards the door in a vain attempt to close it.

He was embarrassed and felt helpless. He wasn't even sure how long they stood there for, sniggering at him and staring, but it had been long enough that he would remember two things. The first was a wish that if only Silvio were there to slap each teenager so hard for what they were doing to him. He thought of how his father would inflict real pain upon the bastards. And the second was that he would now stay away from public restrooms. Forever.

He wondered why he was still watching the damned film. It brought nothing but bad memories, fear and a tightening to his chest. In his delirium, he was afraid that this fear might even come alive in some horrific form, but he was unsure how. Yet – and an amateur shrink might have soon isolated and diagnosed what was the true root of this panic - it was the anxiety of what he had do that night that kept him glued to his uncomfortable position.

It was Sunday. For most it meant closed stores and religious duties, but to him it was an inescapable hell, perpetuated by the education system of Greater Toronto. He had an assignment given to him every Friday by his teacher. Her students had to write down what had happened to them that weekend. This should have been a simple enough task.

The credits rolled on the movie. Wisecrack after wisecrack, but not from him.

The lights in the basement were turned on.

He, though, remained motionless, his gaze still transfixed on the dark screen. Finally, it was his father who came and collected him, ushering him out of his frozen state on the floor.

Half an hour later, he went upstairs to the main floor of the bungalow. The modest home only had the two floors. He reluctantly headed down the hall and into his room to start his journals, passing the small bathroom on his right and his sisters' bedroom on his left. His room was farther down, nearest his parents'. The walls of the hallway were busy with family photos.

A Toronto Maple Leaf game was on in the living room, and his father was watching. He could hear the announcer enthusiastically herald Wendel Clark's performance, "What a shot and goal by Wendel!"

He wished he could watch. He loved Wendel Clark. But he had other things to do.

Instead, he shuffled reluctantly to his small room, leaving the door ajar so he could hear the game.

There was no desk in his room, so he had to sit on his bed. The headboard was an oak steering wheel, and he had blue sheets with seagulls. The wallpaper of the room had little blue boats on it, and this made him feel safe. Something about blue, and something about water, was peaceful to him. Peaceful and clean and able to cleanse.

And yet there were those other times, those mischievous and mean hours when he was scared, and so anxious that he crawled like a thief in the night to under a sister's bed. Both girls disapproved, and so he trained himself to be silent in his stealth. If caught, he would be despatched back to the hell of his own room.

He grabbed the backpack next to him. The black bag was already open. It seemed to be taunting him. He took a red notebook from inside and opened it up. It didn't matter where he opened it up. Not a single page had been written on.

He then reached inside his backpack and took out a pencil.

He put the tip of the pencil to the top of the page to write, but no words came. His soul had nothing to offer him. He was an empty vessel. Instead, he felt only that same sense of doom he had felt downstairs while watching that creature pull that man into the swamp.

I can't do this, he thought.

He owed his teacher something, and yet could not produce a thing. He could have written about anything and anyone. He could even have written about the film and how much it terrified him. All he could produce in the end though was a single scratch of the pencil, accidently drawn as the result of a nervous shake from his hand.

From the living room, he could hear the announcer once again praise Wendel's performance.

"Isn't he having a night for the ages?"

Wendel Clark would never have such problems. He could write in a journal easily.

If only I were more like Wendel, Joey thought.

Nothing bad ever happens to him.

Nothing like the bad things that will happen to me.

Chapter 2

Things could have been so different for Joey. He could have been a professional. As Brando famously said, "I coulda' had class. I coulda' been a contender. I could've been somebody."

But let's not rush ahead...

Soccer brings people together. You can be anyone from anywhere, but if you have a soccer ball and a patch of turf, asphalt or concrete, one can escape into another world. The game is supremely democratic, a great leveler. Brazil, Africa, China, Germany. Sao Paulo, Athens, Naples, Tokyo. All threaded together by a name on a shirt or a game on the TV in a bar.

He was a soccer player. A good one. He wasn't primarily interested in lifting trophies. He was good enough to earn people's praise for his skills. Yet it wasn't praise that was the most important thing young he received during those summers from the age of seven to thirteen. He experienced utter freedom and unfettered boyhood joy, and so much that he forgot about piffling anxieties like his schoolwork. There was the liberty to kick a ball around and relish the thrill of it being slipped mischievously (and somewhat skillfully) in-between and through the goalkeeper's legs. There was the freedom to join his friends by the old pitches, Marco and Roberto, at their picnic table, and the absolute comfort of familiarity that this perpetual and perennial invitation brought. He and anyone who wished it enjoyed a bowl of hot pasta, fresh from the gargantuan steel pot sitting on a nearby table. The food was prepared by Silvio, the Italian male nudging the missus out of the kitchen. *"You do ok, but hey, this is serious now."*

Sometimes Marco's dad cooked. Sometimes, it was Roberto's. They were all good, but Joey was biased. He preferred his own father's cooking.

Soccer was everything to him. It was something, a love, not tangible or huggable like a parent, and yet just as pivotal to his boyhood. He recalled sitting there under the shade of the tree by the field, eating *insalata di funghi* or *porcetta; ziti* or *manicotti,* prepared by any one of the fifty or more mothers to the extended soccer family that congregated there.

He looked around him from the comfort and security he sensed under that willow – it is tough to be anxious sitting under a weeping willow - and looked across the six other games. He felt his team could beat any of the other teams.

He had already played his first game of that day, with two more on the schedule, fuelled by the carbs perpetually on offer. The sun was high in the sky, and not a cloud in sight to think about blocking it. Other times she dipped until they played in the fading light and beyond. There were days of sudden tornadoes, vicious headwinds, summer downpours, and sunburns.

Here he ruled. Even at school, where his grades were supremely ordinary, his quick wit and complacent countenance allowed for a swagger, and yet this was different. Here he flourished. And he knew it, but without forcing others to distaste. Rather others wanted Joey on their team, bossing the game from the engine room of the midfield. He was also always keen for the glory of the goal-scorer. He was not idiotic enough to be that magnificent eccentric type, the goalkeeper, but also gladly took the role of provider and grafter.

He soared out there on the green baize with its brown and grassless goalmouths, and it felt so good, given his academic failings. That

National Geographic documentary showed the growth of the young boy, evolving into sporting talent, the instinct telling him and his caring parents where a future, a vocation, a career for the lad may lie. If he were to survive on those harsh plains, this may prove to be the natural and instinctive strength, upon which he was to rely in life.

✧

Many evenings, he played on the field at the back of his house. He would play by himself, testing his right foot on crosses and shots, never seeming to tire. The energy and the imagination of the youth inspired by sport can lead to a frenzied enthusiasm. The permutations a ball may take, its trajectories and velocities versus the goal stanchion and opponents inspire in the budding player something we call the *Glory Boy*. And the Glory Boy will chase a ball when no sane person would be bothered, for in the tackle, the play, the shot, the goal – in the last minute – we find utter ecstasy. The Glory Boy knows how it feels when everything falls into place, and it is always worth the extra ounce of effort. This is primordial, and unchanging over generations. And it prods at emotions in the young male that none of us can really explain. And the thing about glory is that it is supremely addictive.

He played for the Woodbridge Strikers. The club was noted for its never-say-die attitude, from the junior teams all the way up to the youth and full squads. It was perhaps the tough and masculine European stock – many escaping war and tyranny -, from which they drew in their catchment area, types who had the game deeply etched in their psyches. Each player was an important cog in the machine, and they relied on each other as the fellow *émigrés* had to when they first landed in the New World. The parents came to support and cheer their boys on. The team uniforms were a bright and clean white like the teeth in a dentist's commercial or a new-improved soap powder's effects on muddy t-shirts. The kits were always spotless at kick-off, and the profoundly defiant and proud mothers made sure of this. The club emblem was a shield with a red and white soccer ball in the middle, a Canadian maple leaf jutted out from the top of the shield. 'Woodbridge Strikers' was proudly displayed below.

✧

When he heard Silvio's famed whistle – that bizarre and piercing kind that some men can do without a finger, teeth slightly over the bottom lip and maximum volume – he knew his old man was in the vicinity. At practice, he knew he had to stop joking around when he heard it. When it was witnessed at games, he knew he had to step up the pace, grab the game by the scruff of its neck.

But it was a referee's whistle that blew in the distance, and his daydreaming was over. He jogged over to his dad and handed him his empty plate. Joey ran back out onto the pitch, players from the opposing team making their way onto the turf and into their position.

Joey Tomaselli was happy. His stage awaited.

✧

We now turn from his sporting sanctuary to a pivotal boyhood episode which, like *Swamp Thing*, the vicious attack by the neighbour's dog and the humiliation in the public bathroom stall, might be seen as brutal and guilty parties in the formation of young Joey's mental demons and nemesii.

It was 1993. his hero Magic Johnson had just been diagnosed with HIV...

It is the ancient Egyptians that are credited with 'inventing' the celebration of birthday parties. It started as a coronation for kings, who, when crowned, became seen as gods to the people. It was then the Greeks, who rightfully decided that some kind of dessert would go best with such an event. Thousands of years later, the tradition remains, and it is now the Italian family, the Tomasellis, who honor their middle daughter, Nadia, and her sixteenth birthday.

The event, though not as extravagant as an Egyptian coronation, was still a joyous one. Every table had bone-white balloons attached to the legs. Some had managed themselves loose and instead floated untethered at the ceiling of the single-storey *Ciociaro Social Club*. Chicken wings, pizza and chips were abundant on several foldout tables. There was, of course, a large birthday cake at the end of one of the tables, segregated from the other foods. A one and a six stood neatly together side by side on top of the cake. It had already been cut into pieces and was ready to be served.

He loved that his sister Nadia encouraged – even urged and begged - him to attend her party. He hung out with his sister's friends by the dance floor, as the brooding older boys looked on with the intensity of young bulls to the drone of inoffensive *Billboard* hits.

He wore denim jeans and a James Dean t-shirt. His haircut was in style, *alla moda*; short on the sides, long on the top.

There were around forty people there, and he knew all of them. He remained within the amorphous group, adjusting to the flow of the small cluster as it moved from dance floor edge and then to the car park to puff on illicit cigarettes.

The fresh-ish September air greeted the small cluster of friends, as they exited one more time. They faced the parking lot where Fiats, Camaros, and Cadillacs were neatly parked. A few adults from the party leaned against their cars and smoked too. They turned away with clemency, so as not to have to admonish and scold the kids.

He took a few steps away from the kernel of the group and walked to a discarded and partially wrinkled bag of potato chips that had been dropped on the ground. The bag was half-full. He picked it up, pondered for the briefest moment. Then, viscerally and to no logic, he reached into the bag, took out a chip and ate it.

His sister's friend, a short girl with pigtails, shrieked in mock disgust.

"You're going to get AIDS!" she said, laughing, pointing, exposing.

The other kids in the group chimed in with their hyena cackles, as well.

He did not laugh.

The girl meant nothing by it. It was an innocent joke, or she meant it as such.

He looked down at the bag in his hand with wide eyes and a twisted grimace.

Oh my God, what have I done? he thought. Magic Johnson! Noooooooo!

Had he achieved the impossible? Had he contracted AIDS without even the joy of coitus? Had he plumbed the depths of humanity and would he now die, in infamy, and ignominiously cut down before his prime by a potato chip?

Life had been so kind to him for years, since the horror of his homework anxiety and the sanctuary of sleeping under his sisters' beds. He had been lost in a fine whirling oblivion of soccer balls, loved ones, laughing pals, *porcetta* and summer glory. That all ended in that car park that day. Life can be so fragile, and now the vertebrae of his very existence - those warm boyhood days with golden midges in a dropping tangerine sun and no pain – as well as his once-ebullient psyche suffered a hairline fracture.

He could barely find the strength to move. His sister's friend looked over to him with narrowed eyes.

"Are you okay, Joey?" she asked.

He looked up from where his gaze had wandered to a spot on the grass.

"Yeah, I'm fine," he replied, taking off towards the inside of the party.

"Well then, where are you going?" she said.

Without turning around, Joey replied, 'To wash my hands.'

The others thought nothing of it.

But he was already damaged...

A phobia is an irrational fear of something that's unlikely to cause harm. The word itself comes from the Greek word *phobos*, which means *fear* or *horror*.

Hydrophobia, for example, literally translates to fear of water.

When someone has a phobia, they experience intense fear of a certain object or situation. Phobias are different than regular fears because they cause significant distress, possibly interfering with life at home, work, or school.

People with phobias actively avoid the phobic object or situation or endure it within intense fear or anxiety. Phobias are a type of anxiety disorder. Anxiety disorders are very common. They're estimated to affect more than thirty per cent of U.S. adults at some time in their lives.

—www.healthline.com

The old TV was showing a Sunday evening movie when they got in and they all retired down to the basement with the family. The film was called *After the Quake*.

Credits.

It is October 16th. The 1989 World Series is at Candlestick Park to host the local rivals from across the bay; San Francisco and Oakland. The vast open stands are bathed in late summer early fall evening sunshine. It is a perfect sporting and municipal scene. It feels as if the whole world is watching the neighbors about to clash, slug it out over the garden fence. The TV host welcomes millions with a backdrop of the lucky thousands in their seats. The picture flickers. The voice comes in and out. The screen goes black. And silent.

The top deck of the Cypress freeway collapses on the highway below, and forty-two lives are lost. The 1906 quake had taken thousands of lives, but not from the tremors themselves. The wooden structures of old had gone up like a tinderbox and most lives then were taken in the ensuing fire. This is a modern city, and the peril of wood is now the weight of concrete and the danger of glass and gas.

None of this worries him, until he sees a bloodied leg under a metal girder.

And in a flash, sporting and social beauty on that sublime Californian evening turns to abject horror.

Blood. Blood. HIV. AIDS. Death. My death. My sorry and ignominious death.

Impulsive-Compulsive Disorder (OCD) is a brain and behavior disorder that is categorized as an anxiety disorder in the Diagnostic and Statistical Manual of Mental Disorders, Fourth Edition (DSM-IV). OCD causes severe anxiety in those affected and involves both obsessions and compulsions that interfere with daily life. Research suggests that OCD involves problems in communication between the front part of the brain and deeper structures. These brain structures use a chemical messenger called serotonin. Pictures of the brain at work also show that in some people, the brain circuits involved in OCD become normalized with either serotonin medicines or cognitive behavioral therapy (CBT).

He had washed his hands three times in the last hour, each time for at least ten minutes. It wasn't because he was nervous about kissing Cathy, the pretty brunette with the great smile. It was ever since he had eaten that chip, and not a day, barely even an hour, had passed when he wished with all of his being that he hadn't done that. Now, he wondered what germs swam around inside her welcoming mouth.

'Are you ready?' Cathy asked, her right hand playing with a long strand of her hair.

He was. Women didn't scare him. He had planned to French kiss her, and he would.

The two stood on the side of a large open field. It was recess. A few kids were around but none were too close to see the intent in their eyes. The sun was shining down on both of them, and he admired her perfect olive skin.

He leaned in. He took Cathy's hand. Their lips locked first, and then their tongues touched. It was more sloppy and slimy than pleasurable. Yet at the same time, it was intimate.

In-between the kissing as they caught their breath, she murmured something, her face barely concealing a shy and aroused smile. He misinterpreted her gesture, and accidently bit down on her tongue. She reeled back. It was more surprising than painful though, and she quickly recovered. He felt a weird sensation flash through his mind. He was reminded immediately of the chip.

"Am I going to get AIDS now?" he spat.

Cathy laughed loudly. She was sure that he was making a joke. She knew he was funny. It was one of the reasons she liked him.

His mouth remained impassive. He was staring into her eyes, waiting for an answer. Not sure what he wanted, Cathy replied simply, "No, Joey. You'll be fine."

He felt some small relief, but still, he couldn't erase the worry.

Did she *have to* tell everyone?

He laughed along with them though because what else could he do. He knew it sounded silly too. But he couldn't stop his own rampant and unleashed thoughts. It was too late. Something seemed to inhabit him now, and at thirteen, he didn't have a name for it.

He wanted to call it something. He wanted the worries to go away, fade worry-free like that tangerine sun of his youth.

Where he had once found a shield behind the Woodbridge team crest, he was now thrust into a frenzied and soapy ritual of self-protection at kitchen and bathroom taps and under shower heads.

When Silvio's patience snapped, he tried to make him understand that nothing would happen to him if he did not scrub to the point of pain, and that all these extra showers and hours of hand washing were testing Silvio's patience.

22

One night, Silvio brought him to the bathroom.

'Clean the seat!' he said and handed his son some toilet paper. 'Nothing will happen to you.'

He, however, was paralyzed with fear, especially when Silvio told him to go to bed without washing his hands. He sat in his bed with his hands raised in the air ensuring they wouldn't touch a thing.

He waited an hour for Silvio to fall asleep, in the hope that he could finally wash his hands. When he thought it was safe to go, he got up and moved quietly. Silvio was waiting. That night, he lashed out at his son. With words not his fists. Silvio had meant well, but he just couldn't comprehend the torment in his son's mind.

He still found refuge on the sports field. Soccer may not have been able to answer his questions as to why he felt so concerned, but it *was* able to provide him with a healthy escape.

He hoped that nothing would ever get in the way of his love of soccer.

At thirteen, he couldn't imagine a life without it.

Chapter 3

The foibles of youth can cloud the truth. Time plays tricks. We think we will live forever. We believe if an opportunity is missed or passed up, another will trundle our way long before sunset. Well, foibles is as foibles do... And youth, well, we now know *that* it is wasted on the young.

They were in the waiting room.

He fidgeted in his seat. He looked down at his hands, inspecting them for something- anything that could be considered dirty.

'It'll be okay, *amore,*' Mary said as she placed her warm hand on his. 'It'll be okay.'

He wasn't convinced. Neither had been his father. Silvio didn't think any son of his needed a therapist.

However, it had been neither of their choices. Mary had seen the evidence of his anxiety mount, with the constant hand washing and showers. She had decided it was best for him to get help.

'Joey, Joey Tomaselli,' the receptionist called. 'The doctor is ready to see you now. You can go on back.'

Mary ushered him up and herded him through a door, and then

through a narrow hallway and to the doctor's office. There was just a wooden desk, a small chair, a full bookshelf, and a couch.

Joey and Mary sat down together, side by side on the sofa, while the doctor, whose name he quickly forgot, was across from them, a little pad and pen in his hand. He was a tall man, Indian, and with an engaging gaze.

'So, Joey. Why can't you seem to stop washing your hands?'

'I don't know.'

'Do you feel you have to wash your hands all the time? Can you force yourself to stop?'

'No, I can't. I'm always worried that I might get sick.'

The doctor took a moment to think.

'I understand. It sounds like what you need are prescription drugs.'

'I heard those things have side-effects,' he said, protesting and using that term he had heard Silvio mutter.

'Yes, what about the side-effects?' Mary said.

The doctor acknowledged their concern.

'They may cause a slight physical and mental slowness, but they might really help your son's anxiety.'

'I can't take those then. I have soccer,' he said.

He didn't want to give up one of the last freedoms he had. He did not want to blunt his one true joy.

January 15th, 1994.

It was a significant day. Perhaps more than significant. More like pivotal. He was waiting outside the youth club for a cab, the birthday party was over. He had his hands dug deep into his pockets, as the frosty wind whipped around him harshly.

Hurry up. Where are you?

He was nearly fourteen, and a year had passed since his one and only session with the therapist. He was a handsome teen, and the girls in the rec center had known it. He thought about them as he stood out in the cold, and it was enough to block out the elements from his thoughts momentarily.

A tangerine and green taxi pulled up in front of him. The driver waved for him to get in. He opened up the back door of the sedan, the welcome warmth from the car's heater hitting him.

"'Sup?" he said.

The cab driver answered, 'Hey! What's up?'

'Nothing much, man.'

He gave the address of where he was going.

Five minutes earlier, he had been offered a joint for the first time in his life. He had accepted, taken a hefty tug on it, and was now on the precipice of a brave new world.

The driver began talking about something, but Joey's mind was now somewhere else. Physically he was still riding around in a taxi in Greater Toronto and heading home. However, on the inside, he felt something shift around, and the pieces of his mind - and the peace of mind that had eluded him - began to fall into place. There was now a mellow haze, and – quite marvellously - he could feel the anxieties melting away.

His mind began to fade to black, and a new process of thinking started to take place, something much more lucid. The thoughts now flowed across his consciousness like words from a script on his mind's eye, and he read them to himself. Joyously.

Then, without warning, Joey suddenly blurted out, 'Wow, I'm really thirsty.'

The cab driver started laughing, so out-of-the-blue was his loud and tangential blurt.

'Okay, we can stop a corner store,' he said, putting her signal on to turn left. He changed lanes and drove towards Mac's Milk Convenience.

He pulled up in the small parking lot.

'OK, be right back' Joey said, already getting out of the car, with his mind focused only on one thing.

He suspected the fella knew he was high but was not seasoned enough to be paranoid. Just floating, high, oblivious. And thirsty.

He opened the door, and immediately headed towards the back of the store where the drinks were. He paced back and forth until he found what he was looking for, and then opened one of the frosty doors and grabbed a large bottle of apple juice from the rack. It was ice cold. He unscrewed the lid, put the mouth of the bottle to his lips, and began chugging. The drink washed over his sandpapery throat.

'Ahhhhhh!'

He couldn't help, but let the sigh slide out. He felt good. He felt very good. More importantly, he felt relaxed. He felt in control. In a groove. He didn't need to do a thing, and he was happy to just stand there with his empty bottle. There was no desire to wash or clean himself, and no anxiety to make him feel restless or to invade his thoughts with ideas of catching some unknown cold or virus. There was just a mellow rapture and a sense of peace. He welcomed in a sublime euphoria.

He finished it, took another and walked to the register, so she could pay. He then headed back into the car.

He chuckled happily to himself, but he had found something much more, and something that took all the pain of his existence away. He wasn't about to let it go that easily. There was something far more illuminating on his moistened lips and that was a vast smile.

Half an hour later he was home.

He walked through the quiet hallway, unzipping his coat. His sister was already in her room, and their parents already asleep. He too wanted to sleep. It was all his body craved to do.

He skipped the bathroom ritual, ignoring it in its entirety. He felt no need to wash and scrub himself. There was no inner force pushing him to do it. He could let go.

Oh god. This is amazing.

Once inside his room, he threw his jacket across the bed and quickly changed into his pajamas. He then slid under the covers with one easy motion. He wanted nothing more than to just sleep, and for the first time in years, he slumbered peacefully. The only thought he had thought before drifting off to sleep was a reminder for the future:

*This is **the** answer. I've got to get some more of that stuff. This is **the** answer.*

✦

'Would you care for anything else to drink?' the stewardess said to the father and son in a strained English accent.

Silvio replied, 'No,' and Joey shook his head. She smiled and went to assist the couple behind them.

The plane was carrying them to Italy. It was September 1996. Bill Clinton was about to be re-elected, and Tupac had been shot and killed. Also, Joey's talent as a soccer player had been discovered.

He was the star player at the Woodbridge Strikers. His friend Roberto and he had been asked to play for the Ontario provincial team. It was a true honour, and hie relished the stage. He was not over-awed, but instead sensed he was moving towards his destiny.

Silvio still had connections in Italy, in his hometown of C_____, a small village an hour from Roma. And so, he was able to get scouts from the nearby town of L___ to come and look at his son play in Canada. L___ was big enough to have a club in *Serie B,* the second rung of the Italian league, and when they saw him play, they offered to take him on a month's trial back in Europe.

Silvio made the necessary preparations. He paid for the flight, and even took time away from the car shop. He was invested. It wasn't easy to take time away from work. It was the main source of income for the family, but for his boy's future, it was worth it.

Joey was excited. He wondered where he would be playing and what kind of coach he would have. In Canada, he had been playing in Lamport Stadium, Rainbow Creek or at Centennial Park. These were places that made playing the game fun and easy with their billiard baize surfaces. But soon his mind was elsewhere. He wondered where on earth he was going to score weed. The drug that had become his best friend for the past two years had also become something upon which he depended. He really couldn't do anything worthwhile without it.

Since he had discovered his crutch, he had been smoking two to three joints every day. It reduced his anxiety and made him feel secure. It was his self-prescribed medicine. Thinking about his supply of weed made him feel a slight unease inside his chest, as he shifted in his seat. His bowels were on edge.

'Is everything all right?' Silvio asked.

'Everything's fine, Dad,' he replied.

Silvio smiled. He was proud of his son. He wouldn't say it, but it was true.

His son would make him proud in Italy. He just knew it.

An hour later, the plane descended into Rome's Leonardo da Vinci-Fiumicino airport. They came in over the sea, it was cloudy and therefore were robbed of the chance to try to spot famous landmarks from the sky. As they had done so many times, the pair found new avenues to chat excitedly about their hopes for the trials. He would be given two weeks to prove himself to the manager. They both knew it would be tough.

They were picked up outside the Arrivals terminal by his uncle, G_____. He helped load their luggage into the trunk, and then hopped into the back of the small Fiat. The outskirts of Roma offered no hint as to the history of the city, and they drove out to the country-side. Apart from one day trip to the Olympic Stadium to watch Lazio play Parma, they missed out on the Colosseum, Saint Peter's Basilica, the Vatican, the Spanish Steps, the Pantheon, the Tiber and the plazas. They did not throw a coin into the Trevi fountain and make a wish. Perhaps he – or more to the point, perhaps Silvio - should have.

The trip to the countryside was peaceful, even banal. He couldn't understand what his father and uncle were saying for the entire ride, but it didn't bother him. The only thing that concerned him was the looming question of where he would get weed. He was more worried about that than how good he would do the next day at practice.

When they got to the town of L_____, he found it engaging and quaint. It was a small town with many two-storied detached neighborhood homes nestled together. A river snaked its way through part of the ancient town. Where Joey would be staying though was up a big hill, away from the center. Joey's uncle drove up the incline for a few kilometers until they came to a long driveway. They parked in front of a sizable home with a large backyard, overlooking the town. The house was a three-storey structure with a Tuscan-styled roof of dark brown terra-cotta tiles. Off from the long driveway, one could see animals off to the side of the house, a few dozen yards away. He observed a couple of cows yawning and munching on the grass.

Silvio and his son helped get the luggage out of the back of the car, and brought it to the door, where his aunt and his two cousins stood. His aunt, Antonia gave him a big hug and said something in Italian he couldn't understand. He waited for his father to translate before responding. Afterwards, he greeted his cousins, one boy, Mercantino and one girl, Tiziana. Their English seemed to be a little better.

With the happy reunion having taken place, he was shown to his room. It echoed, as it was roomy, and had everything he needed. Well, not everything but he couldn't expect to find weed waiting for him in his aunt and uncle's house.

He unpacked his things and went to join his family in the kitchen. His aunt had food waiting for them. He was hungry and took a seat next to his father. For now, he could forget about weed and focus on lunch.

There would be plenty of time to find weed.

The next day, he was standing in front of his new coach, Dino, a tall and skinny man with gaunt features and dark hair. A translator called Luigi stood next to him and interpreted what the man was saying. Silvio was a few feet away, talking to the manager of the team, Alessandro.

'It's nice to meet you,' his coach said. This was the extent of his English. Joey replied in kind, and the coach began to explain – in

Italian - to him what would happen. He handed him an all-green uniform and the translator told him to put it on. His training was to begin. He waved to his father, and headed off with the coach, who led him into the locker room. Once inside, he got changed quickly and then met the coach and the translator back outside. The coach gave him a look over, checking his calves and thighs and nodded to himself. He then gestured to Joey to follow him, where he then introduced him to the rest of the team *en masse,* and who were all practicing on the field.

Joey raised an open palm to the team, but they barely acknowledged him. He knew right away that he was the outsider, and that he wasn't welcome. It made him miss home, and it made him remember that soon he would have had a semi-formal coming up that he had been eager to attend. He hadn't been doing the best in school, in-part because of the weed, but he still looked forward to some things about his education. He should have been concentrating on the training, but he was immediately on the defensive.

The coach got him into the session. The field wasn't as nice as the one back in Canada. It was mostly dirt and had patches of grass mixed with what looked like some type of sand. Joey wasn't impressed.

Then the coach blew the whistle and explained what would happen. The translator interpreted for Joey, who found out he wouldn't even be touching a ball for the first three days. He was to run drills. The coach sent him to an obstacle course of hurdles and told him to run over them. He wanted to test his stamina and endurance.

He did as he was told, with the bright sun beating down on his neck and face. It didn't take long to work up a sweat.

By the end of the day, he was worn out. The sun was setting, and all he wanted to do was find some weed but he couldn't just ask his cousins, not out of the blue. He didn't want anyone to know he was smoking weed. Once back at his aunt's, the best he could do that night was sneak Wilson cigarettes from his uncle's pack, and smoke them when he could. More than anything, he didn't want Silvio or his uncle to catch him in the act.

The next two days went very much the same. He showed up for

31

practice and ran drills. The other players barely regarded him, and by the end of the day he was exhausted. He had never been put through his paces like this.

✧

At night, he looked for weed. He would go out around the town, asking strangers if they knew where he could get some.

'*Erba! Marijuana! Prego.*'

Each responded the same; that they couldn't help him. Sometimes he would go out with his cousins to the bars, and try there, but still, he came up empty-handed. He was in a strange place and had no idea what he was doing. Even the women knew he wasn't from there and regarded him in the same fashion as his would-be teammates.

✧

When he finally got the chance to kick a ball, he was ecstatic. It was an opportunity to prove what he could do. He found his new coach to be tactical, and after only five days, he could see himself vastly improving. The drills were working.

His moment of apparent truth came when a rival team from a nearby town came to visit, and he got his chance. He scored two neat goals in a three-one victory. He celebrated alone with a fist pump, as his colleagues jogged back to their own half. His teammates were happy to win, but it seemed they still felt Joey to be an outsider. And so, he was again reminded of the times he would sit around his basement. He felt comfortable there. Nostalgia was taking a hold, and this is not helpful for a teenager, who should be ploughing a furrow towards his dream life. Here, in a country where he didn't speak a single word, he felt alone and miserable. He needed weed, and he was afraid that sooner or later, his anxiety would come back.

And this was how his two weeks would pass. During the day, he excelled at soccer and performed as expected. He scored goals at a remarkable rate. The endurance of the extreme physical tests was giving way to Joey being permitted to show this core skill; a thunderbolt shot that could make any of the club's goalkeepers look out of position, unprepared, slow and silly. This rendered his teammates and opponents dumb, loose-limbed and slack-jawed. So, **THIS** was the reason the kid had been brought over from the footballing tundra of Canada. As he had with his weed, he had found his neutral space. This was his spiritual arena, where he could express himself, chuck his shoulders back, thrust his chest forward and hold that chiseled chin high. But despite all the good stuff, the lust for weed and the desire to be a pro were scrapping AGAINST each other within him.

Demons. Here come the demons.

✵

At night, he still scoured the streets, looking for drugs, through back-alleys and around street corners. Each avenue led nowhere useful. The search appeared endless, and no number of cigarettes could give him what he needed. Two years of smoking weed now left him a vicious vacuum to fill. The need to find his fix was raging, and it now ate into his ambition.

As his two-week trial was nearing an end, he knew that a place without weed could never be home. He now jones'd, and his desire became his kryptonite. His superpower was wearing off. Doctor Jekyll was close to the edge, his pinky twitched, his eyes darted, a five o' clock shadow was nigh. It was time to flee.

And in the spiritual home of Shakespearean tragedy, we already know this shall not end well.

✵

Two days later, Joey and Silvio sat across from the coach and the manager of the team. The group sat in a moderately-sized pizza restaurant in the town, a favorite hang-out of the players. It was called *Rocco's*. It was a busy enough place, but the four of them had a more private table away from the buzz and chatter. It was not the perfect place of serenity and measured calm to discuss the future, but there was a tray of homemade margarita pizza in front of them. His father talked in Italian with the two men.

With an element of ceremony, the manager took out a contract, and placed it down on the table. It was time for business.

He listened as Silvio translated what the manager was saying. It was fairly simple: He would get paid a lot of money to play for the team. He would live in the town for the entirety of his contract. He sensed Silvio's joy, pride and relief. When the men stopped talking, they all looked to him to observe his euphoria. For this is what usually happened.

He shifted in his seat and wiped a sweaty hand against his leg.

He knew what he had to do for his future. The answer was obvious, and it had been for days now.

'I'm sorry, I don't want to stay.'

Silvio's mouth dropped open.

The coach and the manager's eyes darted back and forth between each other, their mouths agape.

'What do you mean, Joey?' Silvio said, his voice rising with every syllable. '*This* is your dream.'

Joey shook his head.

'I'm grateful for the opportunity, but I just want to go home. I miss it. I miss my friends and Mom.'

And weed, Joey thought.

Silvio couldn't believe what he was hearing. He had done everything to get his son there, and he could do nothing now that his son was refusing to sign the contract.

The trip - and all the money Silvio had spent and *not* earned at the shop – would be now for nothing.

Once the meeting was over, he shook the two men's hands, and thanked them once again. On the way back to his aunt's house, Silvio could speak of nothing, but trying to get his son to change his mind. He had already made his decision though. He wanted what he wanted. Toronto was safe. He knew what he had there. Friends. Family. And his drug. He just wanted to get back.

Silvio would still try several more times that night to get him to reconsider, but the outcome was the same. His mind remained unchanged and unchangeable. Even his aunt and uncle barely said a thing to him. It seemed the only one still holding on was Silvio. Who could blame him?

The next day, they were on a plane back to Canada.

Barely a single word was spoken between the two of them.

Go home, Glory Boy. You had an open goal. You have only yourself to blame.

✧

That same day, he awaited the arrival of his friends. He was eager to see them. The time change had still allowed him a half-day of sunlight. The semi-formal was the following week, and he wanted to talk to them about whom they were taking. He was just excited to go. He wasn't worried about dates.

The sound of the approaching car snapped him from his thoughts. He saw his friends pull up. The driver killed the engine, and stepped out of the driver's side, while two others stepped out from the back.

He moved from the window – where he stood sentry - to the door, opening it for his friends.

One stood at the top step, with two more just behind him, each with a goofy grin.

Their big smiles were wide and almost went from ear to ear.

'Welcome back. Let's go have some fun.'

'Oh yes!' Joey said. But first went to his room, took three large tokes of a potent joint and opened the window to let out all evidence of mischief.

✧

You blew it, Glory Boy.

35

Chapter

I t was 1997. He had just turned seventeen. The summer had rolled in, bringing a particularly sweltering heat wave with it. He was inside his coach's air-conditioned office. He was in his playing uniform, sitting in the chair opposite the man, who was now on the point of determining his sporting future.

'Did you hear me?' he asked.

Joey nodded. 'Yea, you're cutting me and Owen from the team.'

The coach leaned back in his chair and placed a hand over his mouth, trying to hide a solemn look.

"Yes. I'm sorry it had to happen this way. You're an exceptional player, but we have two other guys we'd like to have play for us. Competition for places is really intense. I hope you understand, and the door can remain open."

Oh! he understood all right. It was all about politics. And rank nepotism. One of the two kids being drafted in had the same surname as the damned coach.

'I get it,' he said, standing up from the chair. The two shook hands reluctantly, and just like that, he was no longer playing for the Canadian national team.

He left the office and went to go find Silvio. He found him waiting outside in the car.

Silvio rolled down the window.

'How'd it go?' he asked.

'Got cut,' Joey said.

'Just you?'

He got in the car.

'Me and another player.'

Silvio nodded gently and placed a supporting hand on his shoulder.

'I'm sorry, son.'

'Yep. Me too.'

Silvio encouraged Joey to go say goodbye to his teammates. He was well-liked by the team, and they would miss him, some more than others but all of them would miss his talent. He found Owen also saying goodbye to the others. The two didn't know each other too well, but they had competed together. It seemed only natural for the two to exchange farewells, now bound by the bond of simultaneous rejection,

'Nice playing with you,' Joey said, extending his hand out to Owen.

Owen met Joey's hand with his own, shaking it.

'You too, Joey. Good luck.'

He continued to play for Woodbridge. It was tough to find out he had found his level, but given the imponderable of politics, was he really out of his depth? Or was this just supremely unfair?

He wondered where Owen would end up.

Owen Hargreaves, Joey thought as he walked out of the locker room for the last time.

I wonder if he'll ever make it.

October 1997

Joey sat on the end of one of the hotel beds with his gaze cast out of the window at the parking lot below. His teammate, with whom he was sharing the room, was hanging out on his bed, relaxing. The TV was on, showing a *Bundesliga* game from Germany. Bayern Munich were playing Borussia Dortmund. Within three years, Munich games would be bossed by a young Canadian called Owen Hargreaves. Two years after that, Hargreaves would then star for England on the biggest sporting stage on the planet, the World Cup, as they threatened to win the whole thing in Japan. Owen's partial English heritage allowed for him to represent the Three Lions and flourish and strut, but because of nepotism, he had been considered not good enough for the footballing minnows of Canada. The irony and the frustration were not lost on Joey Tomaselli.

The Woodbridge Strikers had won the Ontario Cup. Joey had excelled and scored the winning goal. So, the team were now in a four-star hotel in British Columbia. It was an opportunity to redeem themselves in the nationals after having lost the previous year. He wanted revenge and the sentiment was shared by all of his teammates.

The team had already won all their games thus far, needing only to beat Saskatchewan to advance to the final.

The idea of winning sent a brief hit of dopamine to the forefront of his brain. He was instantly reminded of his weed.

When was the last time I smoked? Joey thought.

An hour ago?

Joey reached into his jean pocket and fingered the bag of weed inside.

'I'm going out for a bit,' he suddenly announced, standing up from the bed.

His teammate barely reacted.

'Have fun smoking,' he said, his gaze still focused on the TV.

'Oh, I will,' Joey replied.

Silvio and Mary were somewhere in the hotel, and he wanted to avoid running into them. He followed the hallway to the end and took the stairwell down. It exited into a darkened section of the vast parking lot.

A perfect place for him to smoke unseen and unbothered. There were no cars in that part of the lot, and there was a nice grassy bit where he could stand in the shadows and smoke.

He took the baggy out of his pocket and opened it up, taking the pre-roll out. He took his favorite Zippo lighter and flicked back on the ignition and lit the joint, and then placed it in his mouth.

He took a deep inhalation and exhaled even longer. He watched the smoke travel upwards into the darkness, the outside lights narrowly illuminating his spot on the grass.

He was excited to vanquish his rivals the next day. He really wanted it. He also knew he needed a good night's sleep. It was already past ten p.m. The moon was inching closer to its zenith in the sky, and the sounds coming from the various rooms of the hotel had already begun to calm.

He looked down at his burning joint. He could feel the familiar high numb his brain, the pleasure of calming the voices.

After this, Joey thought.

He put the joint back to his mouth and inhaled once again.

After this...

The crowd of perhaps two thousand was chanting. The support was fervent. He stood his ground against an opposing player, coming towards him. They were a goal down. There were just over twenty minutes left in the game. He was tired, but he wasn't yet defeated. He knew he had the energy and the wherewithal left to pull something off.

He went in to tackle him. He committed himself and got a toe to the ball. Had he not reached it, perhaps his spirit would have flagged, but this simple act of reaching something that appeared out of reach energized him. The opposition was not unbeatable. The mind can inflate as equally as she can deflate.

C'mon, Joey! It's yours to take.

The bodies were tiring out there. Such a big game can take its toll on the limbs and the minds of the boys. It is as spiritually draining as it is uplifting. The brain, the soul, and the visceral instinct control and determine the direction in which the burgeoning sportsman goes. He called for the ball.

He looked at the scoreboard for inspiration. Fewer than eighteen minutes left.

This is my stage, he told himself.

In the stands, Silvio and Mary watched their boy.

He was calling for the ball. He was the puppet master in the middle of the field. He was sending it right, left, finding through-balls to the forwards, but the defence held firm. When Saskatchewan did get the ball, and try to break, Joey, still as fit as a lop from his time in Italy and the regime he was exposed to there, would snuff out all attempts at a hiatus from the pressure. He then pushed forward that bit more with the intent of taking shots at goal himself. If his distribution was not allowing his teammates to score, he was going to take the responsibility of doing this himself.

Get in range and let one go!

The Strikers were now beginning to get desperate, as the opposition packed their defence with the whole team. All eleven were now behind the ball. Perhaps a long-range thunderbolt from Joey was the *only* answer.

Ten minutes left.

He collected the ball thirty yards out, just within range, but if he could advance another eight, it would be perfect. He had noticed their keeper favored his left side strongly, so knew which side to target. He moved to pass to the right wing, and the Saskatchewan kid fell for it. He dummied past him, leaving him on his backside. He heard a groan of frustration and mild anger as he left the lad in his wake. The path opened up, and this might be his sweet spot.... *Now!* Silvio knew what was coming, and Mary's hands went to her face. He struck it sweetly, instinctively. Like that Nat Geo wildlife film again. This was not taught. This was what nature – and several thousand hours of practice - had cultivated. He knew it was a goal as he hit it, but he had not figured for the slightest deflection as it passed through the crowded penalty area. A lone, lanky defender stepped blindly into the path of the ball, which brushed his mullet, and sent the goal-bound shot into the inside of the post, and then tamely rolled into the grateful keeper's grasp.

Damn, he thought. So close! Then, pause… Go again!

There was still hope. If he had done it once, he could do it again. Nine minutes, and with no release valve for Saskatchewan – they were no playing with no forwards – there would be more opportunities from the perpetual waves of attack. But alas, nothing would come as close to an equalizer as his long-range shot. That had been the moment.

The whistle blew. It was done.

Woodbridge would be going back to Ontario, once more having lost in the nationals.

There would be no revenge. Not yet. But as any Italian worth his salt will remind you (or if you're unfortunate, just show you) – revenge is a dish best served cold.

January 1998

The Dallas Cup - a youth tournament where some of the best soccer teams from around the world would come and compete – was three months away. It was a big deal and one that often went on to launch careers of major stars.

Despite the loss that Ontario had suffered the previous season, Joey was determined to shine in Dallas. His team had proved them-selves, and as such, had been invited to travel to Texas.

Since he had first heard the news, he had his heart set on a suc-cessful tournament.

He ran drills by himself over and over again, and the coach pushed the team hard too.

The training facility was a huge old aircraft hangar, converted to allow for games during the vicious Canuck winter. The lads were practicing on artificial turf, renowned for giving an odd bounce and being a real bastard, on which to slide-tackle. The burns could be brutal. It wasn't the best condition in which to play, but far more conducive than the harsh tundra of a Canadian January.

He had yet to score a goal, but he knew it was just a matter of time.

Two players from the other team were blocking his path. The ball was at his feet. The goal was in sight. The seedlings of an opportunity were starting to form in his mind.

He made a move.

He began to move left, a small shimmy to fool the defender, but his leg jammed awkwardly in the surface, awkwardly forcing him to suddenly stop short. His knee buckled. He heard a distinct pop. He had heard this in other players, and he had heard too of the career-ending ramifications of knee tears.

He made a hollow grunt. The ball rolled away from him, not that this mattered in the slightest anymore. An athlete knows, in the way a wounded animal in that Nat Geo docco knows.

It took a couple of seconds for the others to notice he had injured himself. When they did though, they stopped play and then helped the now-limping teammate off the field. Not sure what *exactly* was wrong, he sat on the sidelines as the coach ran across to him.

He prayed and hoped it wouldn't be serious. He just didn't want to miss the Dallas Cup. He couldn't bear to be without soccer, nor would he feel good about letting his teammates play without him.

'Are you okay, Joey?' his coach asked, placing a hand on his shoulder.

'I don't know. Something popped. I don't know what.'

There seemed to be a line of worry on his coach's forehead.

'Sit out for now. Make sure you get to a doctor to make sure it's nothing serious.'

He nodded.

'Can you call my parents to come and get me? I don't want to walk home from the club,' he said, his voice strained from the pain he was poorly concealing.

His coach nodded.

'Of course. Absolutely.'

His coach then ran back across the field towards a side office, where he could call.

His teammates looked at him.

'Don't worry, guys. I'm sure I'll be okay.'

Privately, he wasn't so sure.

✦

February 1998

Joey and Mary sat in the tiny office side by side. It had been the third doctor they had been to since the injury over five weeks ago.

The previous two doctors had kindly and efficiently referred him on to specialists in this specific arena. It hurt when he played. It hurt when he didn't play. Of course, weed helped the pain. And allowed him to forget.

The tournament was approaching, and he was desperate to play.

'I am sure we will get some answers,' Mary said.

Just then a door opened inside the office, and the doctor came in with his medical chart.

'Hello, I'm Dr. Simonson. I understand you've got some pain around your knee?'

'That's right,' he said.

The doctor nodded.

'Let's see what I can do. Raise your leg for me.'

He did as he was told while the doctor slipped on two rubber gloves he took from a nearby drawer.

'Okay, let's take a look,' Dr. Simonson said, beginning to prod and examine around his knee. After a few minutes of examination, he leaned back and slipped off his gloves, placing them on the counter.

'Well, everything appears to be fine on the surface, but I know you are in pain. So, let's look for some alternatives,' he said.

Mary said. 'He's in a lot of pain.'

'My knee is beginning to swell. Look!' he said, chiming in.

The doctor observed, intrigued.

✧

March 1998

The Coffee Time training facility was packed. He could just make Mary in the stand to the side, about thirty feet up from the field. Her familiar red hair and warm smile were visible in the sea of faces. Silvio sat next to her and waved to Joey. And he whistled his familiar notes.

Woodbridge Strikers were facing a local rival in an exhibition game.

The game was in full swing. No goals had been scored yet though he hoped to change that. He could feel the swelling in his knee, almost as if it were pulsating, warning him.

He couldn't take heed of it though. He was in the middle of a game.

He began to run forward in a Woodbridge attack.

But he didn't make it far. He slowed, as the ball came his way through the air, higher than he would have liked.

He would have to head it and bring it back down. He jumped and attempted to get the ball. As soon as his leg pushed off the ground, he felt something *SNAP!*

He shouted, and everyone around him stopped. Through his screaming, he could hear Mary's yell as well. It was even more piercing than his. It was a mother's cry.

He crumpled down to the ground in pain. The game was immediately stopped, and the crowd knew what had happened, finally quieting down to hushed tones and murmurs.

The worst that Joey had feared had happened.

✧

Silvio and Joey sat inside Dr. P_____'s office, awaiting his arrival. He was supposed to be one of the best. He treated players from the Toronto

Maple Leafs. Thanks to his connections through Woodbridge, management was able to get him the appointment within a month.

He was hopeful that he would be able to get an answer about his injury.

He hadn't touched a soccer ball since the previous game two weeks before.

'How are you holding up, Joey?' Silvio asked.

'I'm okay, Dad. Nervous.'

Silvio nodded.

The door to the office opened, and Dr. P_____ walked in. Joey and Silvio stood up. He shook both their hands and told them to take a seat.

'So, Joey, I understand you're a soccer player.'

'Yea,' he replied.

Dr. P_____ nodded and took out a pair of gloves from a nearby drawer.

'Take a seat on top of the bed for me, please,' he said, motioning for him to move from the chair.

He did as he was told.

'Now, stretch your injured leg out.'

He again did as he was told.

The doctor took two fingers and placed them underneath his calf. They were there for no more than two seconds.

'Your ACL is torn. I'm sorry to say this, Joey, but you won't be able to play soccer for at least a year.'

The tears were almost immediate. They fell onto and then from his cheek.

His chances of playing in the Dallas Cup were over, as was his participation in the whole season. All that he had hoped for was torn apart in only two seconds. It had been the quickest truth he had ever received. As Silvio could look under the hood of a car and diagnose the precise issue within seconds, then so was this doctor able to pinpoint the precise source of the pain and the problem.

Silvio could do very little but lend his boy his immediate and unflinching support.

He now wept into his own hands.

'I'll give you two a moment, though it is important to know that there will have to be surgery. We can discuss options when I return. But, Joey, we will get you fixed, I will help you feel like brand new, if you're willing to work with me. Excuse me for a moment, please.'

Dr. P_____ left the room, allowing Joey to cry in his own space. It was the polite thing to do. He had seen this scene before.

The good news was that the problem had been found and could be fixed.

✧

July 1998

For the first time in eleven years, he was not playing soccer.

He was distraught most of the time.

But right now, he took solace elsewhere and was high on mushrooms; about a gram's worth. It was his secret, and his friends did not know.

He had decided to take advantage of his free time to go and hang out with Mark and Anthony for the weekend. It promised to be a good time, and he really needed it. The surgery had gone well, though he had to use crutches for two weeks afterwards.

Since the operation in May, he had been bored and restless. Without soccer, there was a void he struggled to fill. He couldn't even visit his teammates, choosing instead to stay away as much as possible, unable to face the truth that he couldn't play for a long time. It seemed that the path of least resistance to pass the time and fill the void with the most fun was drugs. And that weekend was a drugs weekend for him.

His oblivious friends had rented out a motel room next to the property that Silvio had owned when Joey was younger. Silvio had sold it years ago, because the soccer schedule had become more hectic and Silvio had wanted to be a part of it, observe his boy strive for a career again.

Back then the cabin had been a place for the family to escape from the hustle and bustle of modern life.

Now it was a place for him to do drugs and drink cheap liquor. Perhaps bring back a girl or two.

The radio was blaring, and the group nodded their heads in rhythm, their focus on getting ready to go out to the beach.

Anthony sang along to the tunes. The others drank beer and the odd shot of tequila.

'Nice singing,' said Joey, barely able to hold in a chuckle.

Mark laughed, but Anthony kept on singing off-key.

In the middle of the performance and through the window, Anthony could make out two familiar figures approaching outside. He instantly recognized them as Silvio, and his brother, Joey's uncle, Roberto.

'Oh Christ, dude, Joey. It's your dad and uncle.'

He stiffened up instantly.

'What? Are you serious?' he said.

Mark took a peek through the door lens.

'Oh shit, Anthony's right.'

Joey began to panic. He couldn't let his father see him like this, sweating and eyes like saucers.

'Oh shit, what do I do?' he said to his friends. 'I do not want to see them now.'

'Don't worry, we'll go talk to them. Hide here,' Mark said, pointing to underneath the kitchen sink.

'If they come in, they'll never find you here.'

'What? Seriously? Just don't let them in!' he said.

'Where else are you going to go?' Mark replied.

It was true. The floor plan was open, and the room wasn't very big.

With little choice, Joey opened up the sink's cabinets and crawled inside. The space was empty, apart from a few cleaning products and the pipes. Once he was secure, he closed the doors on himself. The power of the mushrooms made the small hidey-hole oddly comforting, and somewhat amusing.

A few seconds later, Mark opened up the motel door, and Anthony and he walked outside. They were warmly greeted by Silvio and Roberto.

'Hey, is Joey here? I thought he would be up this weekend. We wanted to surprise him.'

'Oh, nah. I think he's at the beach or something. He went out a bit ago.'

Silvio's smile diminished.

'Oh, that's too bad. We were looking forward to seeing him.'

'Yea, I bet,' Anthony said.

Underneath the sink, Joey began sweating, because of the heat and his mood changed. It was a tight space, and he couldn't move. Being that high only magnified his fear now.

C'mon guys, get them out of here, Joey thought.

Instead, Mark and Anthony engaged Silvio in conversation for ten minutes, chatting about school and family.

'You guys staying out of trouble?' Silvio said with a grin.

'We're trying, we're trying,' Mark replied.

The four of them shared a good-natured laugh.

'All right. Well, I'll let you guys get back to it. If you see Joey, tell him to drop by,' Silvio said, waving goodbye.

'Will do,' Mark said.

'See ya,' Anthony added.

They watched the pair leave until they were sure they weren't coming back, and then headed back inside, closing the door behind them.

'Okay dude, you can come out.'

Joey opened up the doors and spilled onto the floor.

Anthony and Mark instantly cracked up with laughter.

'Yea, yea, real funny guys. Holy shit. That was close,' Joey said, panting lightly. 'Are they gone?'

'Yea, they're gone,' Anthony said.

He smiled from the floor.

I need a joint, he thought.

February 1999

He felt the bump working immediately. The little white line had done the trick.

"Okay, that's better," he said to himself, adjusting the knee brace underneath his jeans. It was a crude black thing that had been given to him the month before. He had been doing post-op physical therapy at the famous Alan Eagleson Clinic in Toronto since the previous summer. It had been going well, and he was nearly healed.

It was just past ten p.m., and he had already been drinking for several hours at a stag party. He was one of those rare types who could drink and drink and never really show it. The plan was to do some coke and straighten out, so he could have a few more drinks. There was a formula to partying correctly, maintaining the right buzz – a high wire act of perfect ratios - and he knew it well. His pals didn't touch the stuff, only Joey. This was usually fine as it meant there was more for him.

"One more bump," he said to himself, this time just dipping the key into the little bag. He was sitting in the driver's seat of the car, outside the club in the parking lot.

A passing couple, a man and a woman holding hands, eyed him suspiciously as they walked past the car. It only took them a second more to confirm their suspicions of what he was doing, and they immediately pulled out their badges, stepping towards the driver's side window.

He felt his heart sink.

Damn!

The two undercover officers approached him.

"Step out of the car, sir," the male one said.

He did as he was told, leaving the bag of cocaine on the seat.

The male officer motioned for him to take a seat on the curb. Once he had done so, the officer handcuffed him.

"Do you have some I.D?" he asked coldly.

Despite being cuffed, he took out his wallet out of his trouser pocket, and produced his fake I.D.. He was eighteen years old, and the clubs he was going to were for nineteen-year-olds and over.

"A fake I.D *and* cocaine? This isn't looking good for you, Joey," the officer said. "Is Joey your real name?"

He nodded.

"You may as well just kill me now. My dad is going to kill me, when he finds out anyway," he said to no one in particular.

The female officer frowned.

"Should I write it up?" she said to her colleague.

"Sure, that would be great. I'll search the car," he replied.

He felt sick to his stomach. He began to plead with the female cop.

"Please don't do this. This is going to ruin my life. One mistake and I'm going to regret it for the rest of my life. Please."

The male officer ignored him entirely, continuing to scour the car for more drugs.

It's useless.

The woman continued writing the ticket, but then put the pad down and looked into his eyes.

"Look. There's nothing I can do. You broke the law. But I can give you my number in case you need help."

There was a hint of sympathy in her voice. Perhaps she didn't want to see him suffer.

"Okay," he said, with little other option.

She nodded and finished writing the ticket. She ripped it out of the pad and flipped it over, writing her number down on the back.

"Here," she said, handing him the ticket.

"You'll have to appear in court."

He grabbed the ticket with a shaky hand. He couldn't believe he had been caught. It's always something you think will happen to someone else, he thought.

"Okay, all clean," the other officer said, adjusting his shirt.

He walked over to Joey and removed the handcuffs and handed him back his car keys.

He was surprised that he was given back his keys and not breathalyzed, but he wasn't about to say anything. Why ruin what good luck he did have going for him.

"Drive safely," the female officer said. "Call me any time."

She watched him, for a moment more before leaving.

He stood there lamely, watching the two officers walk away.

He felt like crying but couldn't bring himself to do it.

He got into the car. The buzz had gone, but at least he wasn't going to jail.

March 1999

"The case is getting thrown out," the officer said over the phone. It had been the tenth call they had in the past month.

He couldn't believe it. The cocaine bust wasn't going to ruin his life. Silvio didn't even need to know.

"Really?" he said. He couldn't hold his excitement back.

"That's right. The Crown has dismissed the case. You're all clear."

He silently celebrated by making a fist and pumping it towards the sky.

"Thank God. Thank you so much for calling to let me know. You've been a huge help."

"You're welcome," the female officer replied.

"But before I go, can you promise me one thing?"

"Sure," he said.

"Stop doing drugs. You were lucky, but you might not be again."

He could feel she was worried about him. It was genuine concern. He thought she was a good person.

"I will, and I know. Thank you again, officer."

He hung up the phone and immediately breathed a deep sigh of relief.

He wondered whom he was going to tell first.

A week later, he was sitting in his car in a near empty factory parking lot. It was nighttime.

He was enjoying a joint.

"Man, you sure are lucky to have gotten out of that with no record," he said out loud to himself after exhaling a large cloud of smoke.

"Oh, I know," he then thought. His eyes were hazy and out of focus.

"And even luckier that cop had a crush on you," he thought.

He laughed, which quickly turned into a small coughing fit.

A glimpse of blue and red caught his eye from the rear-view mirror. He could make out a cop car approaching.

"Shit," he said, tossing the joint out the window.

He turned just in time to see the red and blue accompanied by a siren.

"Jesus," he said. "Not again."

He could do very little but wait until the cop car pulled up beside them. There were a few tense moments as he awaited his fate. Finally, two officers left the car and made their way to the car.

The officer tapped on the glass with a flash-light so he rolled down the window.

"How are you, sir?" he said, his pupils reacting to the bright light.

"Have you been smoking?"

"Just the tiniest bit. It is medicinal."

"Step out of the car, please," the officer said.

He was strip-searched. The two policemen found nothing.

Fifteen minutes later, he had been admonished and let off with a warning. Somehow – and with an unerring similarity to his coke bust -, he was still allowed to drive home.

Would he never learn?

He had a lot to think about.

April 1999

Dallas, Texas. Finally, he had made it.

The previous month he had scored two goals off the bench. The coach hadn't been sure about his level of fitness coming off an injury, but he proved himself capable, even with the knee brace. He was proud of this. After a year out, he was like a coiled spring, and raring to go.

Now here in Dallas, and after having missed the previous year, was the culmination of his struggles.

A few hours after the team landed, and he was secure in the hotel room, he left to go find some weed. He walked to a nearby gas station and asked a few strangers if they knew where he could get something to smoke. There were a few hard 'No's', but eventually he was able to procure some from a shady looking pair, who took some cash and (perhaps surprisingly) came back with it ten minutes later.

He thanked them and shoved the little baggie into his jacket pocket.

He couldn't wait to smoke it.

'Jesus,' he said, throwing his sweaty jersey onto the locker room floor. 'We should have won that.'

Woodbridge had lost against top English side, Tottenham Hotspur*, 3-1.

He couldn't believe it. He felt that he should have scored in the second half, but he didn't seem to have the speed like he used to. He sensed that wasn't fully recovered yet, and the opposing players had no trouble dispossessing him. He felt he would get that sharpness back. He was maybe seventy-five per cent fit. Many young players are never the same after that first debilitating surgery, but that is usually the out-of-the-blocks acceleration over twenty yards. His style was more of a midfield grafter and it was stamina – not lightning pace - that fuelled his game.

"Hey, it's all right, Joey. You did your best," B_____ said, putting an arm around his friend's shoulders.

"Yea, yea," he said.

---

* The Spurs side that day included Peter Crouch and Jermaine Defoe, future England and world superstars.

He didn't feel much like talking about it. Sometimes, it was just easier to be frustrated and to internalize it.

"We'll win the next one," B_____ said.

He nodded.

"Right. We'll win the next one," he said.

He was amazed at how easy their second game had been going against South African side, Jomo Cosmos from Johannesburg.

The stadium was too big to make out Silvio and Mary, but he knew they were watching him. He had heard Silvio's notorious whistle. He was sure they were worried about him after the tough loss in the last game, and, of course, because of his injury.

It was 2-1 to the Canadians. There were ten minutes left. Although there was only a single goal in it, it felt like an easy victory. There was no late siege on their goal, and they controlled the ball for most of the closing stages. They knew they ought not over-exert themselves with a crucial game to come. But he was already thinking about the next joint through every second of that final few minutes. He ran off the pitch at the final whistle, keen to find his solitude and to get high.

The final game was a major letdown. Before the kick-off, results in other games meant that they could not advance from their own round robin group. This would be the last game.

They were beaten badly. Pumas from Mexico, a crack outfit with a magnificent history in world soccer, thumped them 4-0. Because Woodbridge stood no chance of going to the quarter-final, the coach generously gave the substitutes and reserves a chance to shine, and they were given a game. A second-string Woodbridge stood little chance against the rampant Mexicans. Joey didn't get a game.

Silvio and Mary attempted to console him, but he knew that he could do better, while part of him was grateful to have been there and participating. There would soon be another stage for him.

He had finally made it to the Dallas Cup only to lose.

If only I were playing at 100%, Joey thought.

He was nearly nineteen. He didn't have much time left to prove himself as a would-be professional. Soon, he would be too old to play for the youth teams, and he feared that he would have to put this life behind him.

On the plane ride back, his teammates were quiet.

He sat solemnly looking out the window of the plane, as it landed in Toronto.

June 1999
Baltimore, Maryland

"Yes!" he screamed, as he scored his third goal of the tournament.

Another major youth cup was underway, and this time, he was at his full potential. He knew this was his shop window, his stage.

He was in his pomp, bossing games and as a result, was already being looked at by several prestigious colleges across the continent. He had already been approached by UNLV, Florida State, and South Carolina.

There was real hope.

Again, he took the adulation, hugs, backslaps and hair ruffles of his teammates. It was a good feeling for him to be playing at his best again, back with his friends. Somehow, there seemed less pressure than there had been before. Maybe it had been because the Dallas Cup had always loomed in his mind or maybe he had just grown a bit. Whatever it was, he was far more positive than he had been all year.

There was a nagging doubt in his mind though. His damned SAT's.

If he wanted to get his scholarship playing soccer, he would have to pass the tests, and he had already failed twice. He told himself he still had plenty of time to pass. He just needed to study more, and he promised himself he would; right after he got back to the hotel room and smoked a joint.

After that, it would be study time. Definitely.

October 1999

Woodbridge had again won the Ontario Cup.

It was a bittersweet victory for Joey. Over the summer, he had failed his SAT's seven more times. His ninth and final time had been the month before. School had already started, and he could no longer take the test there. It was too late for that.

More chances blown, Glory Boy.

There was one possibility. In July, Joey and his innocent and oblivious friend, Peter traveled across the border into Buffalo to take the test there. He had been determined in his effort, but the weed he had hidden in the spare tire in the back of the car proved once again to be a foolish distraction. He stayed up late the night before the exam, drinking and smoking alone, so that when the sun did rise over the city, he felt like he could barely keep himself awake. He had made it to the school, but that was it. The result had been another failure.

Now he was too old to play youth soccer. He knew deep down this trip to the nationals was the last time he would be playing with the Woodbridge Strikers. He just didn't want to think about it too much.

Still, he was optimistic about going all the way to the final. He was healthy, and his skills and confidence had improved to new heights.

Why couldn't he win it? Go out on a high note? Maybe catch some club's eye.

Yes, that was what he would do. He would get to the final that year and win.

Together. They would prevail. Perhaps a stunning personal

performance would somehow get him a professional deal without damned school.

✿

They had made it to the semi-final once more. They were one up with ten minutes to go. It was a solid performance, and the boys strutted and swaggered, sensing they were going through.

The constant cacophony of the crowd was like a melody to him, and somewhere in there, Silvio and Mary watched their son proudly. They too were hopeful of a victory.

A freak goal seemed like the only thing that could prevent them.

✿

If one drug bust could not prevent a second the following month, and then still prevent him from smuggling a stash across the U.S. border, then one freak goal could turn into two. The first was straight from a corner kick that should not have been given, and the second a sloppy back-pass from a trusted defender suddenly hamstrung by the pressure of the moment. Top level sport is predominately won and lost in the mind. This time Joey's mind was fine, but one is only as strong as the weakest link. And in a few heart-breaking moments that would replay in young Joey Tomaselli's mind for an epoch, like smoke to hold, it was all over.

And despite the lack of adequate SAT scores, he was smart enough to know *this*. It was instinctive and instinctual. Like that wounded animal in that old Nat Geo docco.

OVER.

✿

The locker room was quiet. Nobody dared speak. The only silver lining in the defeat was that they had lost together, as a unit.

He sat on one of the benches, a damp towel around his neck. He

57

was still in his soccer shirt, even though the game had been over for twenty minutes. He didn't want to let the colors go. He knew he would never wear them again.

His teammates gave each other space. They knew he had lost the most. They knew what Woodbridge had meant to him. He had played for them for twelve years. From the age of seven to nineteen, he had given them everything and even suffered an awful injury because of it. And in a way, Woodbridge had given *him* everything too.

Joey couldn't hold back anymore.

And so, he wept.

With little resistance.

The tears streamed down his cheeks uncontrollably.

There was no more future with soccer.

Over.

Ciao. Arrivederci.

Che bea.

Addio per sempre.

PART TWO

Chapter 5

H e sat at the end of the bar watching soccer highlights on the TV. He noted the players' positioning, fitness, ball distribution, all with the eye of a seasoned coach. It seemed like an outer body experience, his former life was someone else's. Like smoke to hold, it was gone. Some team in red just narrowly avoided conceding a goal against some team in blue. He stared into space instead.

He barely registered the goal when it was finally scored in this turgid affair. His interest in the sport had waned since his dreams imploded on the technicality of a school test.

He had put on weight, and his passion for the game, which had once been a bright spark, was now nothing more than a dull ember.

He now frowned at the TV, took the vodka soda in front of him, and guzzled down the remnants. He motioned with his empty glass to the barman, who nodded.

He was alone, apart from the barkeep and a few fellow college students, who had also decided it was in their best interest to skip class in the middle of the afternoon on a non-descript Tuesday.

He was nearly twenty. He had accepted an offer to play soccer at Humber College in Etobicoke. To fulfill the bureaucratic requirements, they paid for his classes, but he never went to a single one. He wasn't even sure of his major. He thought it had something to do with hospitality. He had forgotten what he had told his parents. The only thing he knew for sure was that if Mary and Silvio found out he wasn't going to class, he would be in big trouble. The soccer was only to run from March to May the following year, so it was all a farce, but a farce that bought him some time.

The bartender brought him his new drink and placed it in front of him. Joey thanked him.

It was late January 2000.

He was officially an adult now, and Silvio had made sure he knew it. His father had looked at his son months prior and told him, "Joey, that's enough now. It's time to get a job."

He couldn't argue.

While he attended college, he worked as a server at *The Sports Club Bar,* a restaurant in Woodbridge. It was his first real work experience, and while it was hard to feel good about serving food and drinks, he met girls and hung out. He also worshiped the owner, Tony, who became a mentor and a wise uncle-type. He was a good-natured older Italian guy with grey hair and a friendly smile. Joey looked up to him, gravitated towards him and wondered what it would be like to have his life. He asked him for advice and tried to tap into his sagacity and worldliness. It meant that staying here was the path of least resistance. For now.

On the TV, the soccer highlights switched to hockey. He took a sip of from his glass and then checked his watch. His class would be over soon. He could go home in an hour and tell Mary and Silvio that his day had been all right and that college was going well.

He looked down at his drink and thought about getting away to somewhere warm.

February 2001

The club played an abysmal sounding mix of Latino and commercial house music that resembled a cacophony of loud bass-drops and shrill FX's. The MC crowed over the top at unseemly intervals.

He didn't care though. He wasn't in Acapulco, Mexico for the local music. He was there to party with his friends.

And get a little high.

Back in Canada, the malevolent and brutal winter had already descended upon Toronto. While he was in Mexico though, the clouds never seemed to obscure the relentless sun and the nights felt just as hot as the days.

He thought of how his life had changed. He was no longer going to Humber College, and now he pondered his old boss, Tony's death, which had saddened him deeply.

Tony's passing seemed to be the physical manifestation of the end of a chapter, and a chapter he was happy to close. No more school. Mary and Silvio *weren't* so pleased, but there was little they could do.

He knew he was wandering, meandering.

Something will come up, he thought. Put myself out there. I can make things happen.

Canada seemed a world away now. A mass of sweaty youth swayed on the dance floor, seemingly in rhythm with the palm trees dotted around the beachfront patio.

He needed a joint.

The friends he had come with were on the dance floor, looking for girls.

He walked away from the crowd towards a more secluded corner. He pulled out a neatly packed joint from his back pocket.

He took a lighter from his other pocket and placed it underneath the tip of the joint and ignited it. He watched the flames work their way around the tip until a nice even burn had started to appear. Once it looked good, he out the lighter away and put the joint to his mouth. He took a big pull and then exhaled deeply as the music echoed around him.

Aaaaaah, that's better.

The bass was loud enough to cause the ground beneath his sneakers to vibrate.

As he relished the moments, he noticed one of the bouncers making eye contact with him. He looked down at the joint between his fingertips. The man shook his head and began forcing his way through the crowd towards him, a large scowl on his face that even seemed to be his permanent countenance.

He began to feel a rush of fear and warm adrenaline. The bouncer was a big bruiser and was through the crowd in seconds.

"You can't smoke in here, unless you pay five hundred dollars, or you will go to jail," he shouted in a thick Mexican accent.

"Oh, okay. I'm sorry, I'm sorry. My friends are over there. They have my money," pointing towards where his friends were hanging out. The security guard followed his finger with his gaze until it came to rest on where he pointed.

"Take me there. Don't try anything."

"I don't want any trouble, please."

He nodded and extinguished the joint on the wall behind him. He then shoved it back into his back pocket.

As he led the bouncer across the room, he had already begun planning his escape. He knew there was a nearby exit to the club, unguarded, that led to out onto the street. He didn't have time to tell his friends. He wished them well, and as soon as he was halfway across the room, he bolted for the exit. Of course, he had not pointed to his real friends.

The bouncer chased him but he was swifter in slipping through the crowd. He had played soccer for most of his life. He wasn't about to be caught by someone twice his size, with fat calves and a paunch.

Out on the streets, he tried to use whatever he could to his advantage. He pushed past anyone in his way, hoping they would slow the bouncer down. He briefly turned his head around and to his surprise saw more than one person chasing him.

Shit, he thought.

He picked up the pace.

His mind was racing almost as fast as his feet were. He needed a solution. Up the ante.

Let's see how much they want me.

He dashed across the busy street, cutting off a few cars and taxis. This bought him enough time to jump behind some bushes and hide. From between the shrubs, he watched as his pursuers ran past him.

God, they'd rip me apart. Look at the size of them.

He waited a few seconds more. When he was certain, he appeared from his hiding place and wiped off the blades of grass and broken twigs from his clothes. He saw them heading off down the main drag.

He sighed. His buzz was gone, and he'd lost his pals. But he was not in jail. And he was not at an ATM, emptying his account for some thugs.

His bed at the Hotel Copa Cabana was a long walk away. He decided a cab would be the safest way to get there.

Drugs: When would he learn?

March 2001

> Hypnosis is a human condition involving focused attention, reduced peripheral awareness, and an enhanced capacity to respond to suggestion.
>
> There are competing theories explaining hypnosis and related phenomena.
>
> *Altered state* theories see hypnosis as an altered state of mind or trance, marked by a level of awareness different from the ordinary state of consciousness. In contrast, *nonstate* theories see

hypnosis as, variously, a type of placebo effect, a redefinition of an interaction with a therapist or form of imaginative role enactment.

During hypnosis, a person is said to have heightened focus and concentration. Hypnotized subjects are said to show an increased response to suggestions.[12] Hypnosis usually begins with a hypnotic induction involving a series of preliminary instructions and suggestion. The use of hypnotism for therapeutic purposes is referred to as hypnotherapy while its use as a form of entertainment for an audience is known as stage hypnosis - a form of mentalism.

—Wikipedia

There are anecdotal tales of miraculous proportions, where the subconscious is revealed like an intact shipwreck in a perilously low tide. This remarkable skill and its wonderous results leave a vast arena for frauds and charlatans. Step with care.

He was sitting in the front row, waiting for the hypnotist to take the stage.

The college pub was packed, with maybe over two hundred people crammed inside. He and his friends had a table and were putting down shots of chilled vodka. Outside it was frigid. Vicious and capricious Toronto was giving a near-final reminder of what she can serve up for winter.

He wasn't sure he believed in hypnotism, but with good friends and liquor, he could deal with pseudo-science.

As the crowd murmured in anticipation, he began looking around.

A few tables away from him, he noticed a spectacular brown-haired girl giggling over a daiquiri glass. Like him, she was sitting with friends. Before he could get a closer look, the lights began to dim, and his attention was drawn back to the stage.

The hypnotist came out from a darkened hallway to the left of the stage. The stage was simple, and perhaps five feet above the ground. Because of this, he could see the man clearly. He wore normal clothes, dressed in a regular shirt and jeans. He wasn't dressed up ostentatiously like these types often are.

On stage, he introduced himself as Gerald and welcomed the crowd. There was no goofy stage name. Joey just didn't believe in this stuff, with or without the gimmicks.

"Hello, everybody. Thank you for joining us tonight, this is a magnificent turn-out. Tonight, I'm going to show you the truly authentic and potent powers of hypnosis and the effect it has on the mind of the individual, using only this gold chain and watch."

The man pulled it from his pocket and let it hang loosely for the crowd to see.

The patrons gave a slight murmur of recognition and awe. Joey said nothing. He only observed.

"For my first performance, I'm going to choose two people at random to come on stage with me.

"But first, I'll need a single chair."

One of the bar-backs grabbed him a wooden stool, handily left by the stage.

The hypnotist placed it in the center of the platform.

"Okay, let me take a look at the crowd."

He scanned the room for anyone.

Joey sat still, watching the man with little expression. If the hypnotist was searching for a pliable visage, he picked the wrong guy.

"How about you, young man?" the hypnotist said.

Joey turned his head around briefly, unsure if the man meant him.

"Yes, you," the hypnotist confirmed.

His friends gave him a nudge.

A few people behind him said, "Go on." "Do it!"

Why not? he thought.

He stood up and climbed on stage. The crowd clapped in support.

"Sit here," the hypnotist directed him. He did as he was told and waited.

"Okay, now I will need a female."

Once more the man scanned the room and pointed at the beautiful woman in the front row. Joey recognized her as the stranger he had watched at a few minutes earlier.

"Yes, you," the hypnotist pointed. She too turned her head in disbelief but was assured by her friends it was she the man wanted.

The crowd clapped as she too climbed on stage. The hypnotist positioned her a few feet in front of Joey.

He waited for the crowd to silence before walking over to the girl until he was between his two guests. He then looked into her eyes.

"Now I am going to hypnotize you. Watch this chain sway back and forth, and the watch at its end. I am going to suggest to your subconscious a specific action. You will then perform this action, with no memory later on if it has occurred. You will be receptive to this process and only stop when I have told you to."

She nodded, already seemingly mesmerized by the man's intuitive eyes.

Joey sat watching the exchange, unsure of what was about to occur. He looked to his friends for encouragement, but they too were transfixed on the hypnotist and what was about to happen.

"Let's begin," the man said.

The energy of the room seemed to shift to one of curious expectation. The enchanter's tone now went from explanatory to directive.

He began to swing the chain back and forth, slowly at first, letting it build momentum.

"Breathe. Breathe deeply. You are feeling relaxed. You are safe. You are free. There is nothing to worry about. You can do whatever you want. You can give this man a lap dance. You will give this man a lap dance. You want to give him a lap dance. You desire to do so."

The hypnotist continued to work the girl. He watched from his stool, as she seemed to lose focus on the crowd around her. Like being engrossed in a movie or book, the outside world seemed to fade away from her. Her eyes widened and a calm expression took hold of her face. Her jaw relaxed and her eyes drooped slightly. Her ample-ish chest began to fall and rise more slowly and deliberately.

"You are giving this man a lap dance. You are giving this man a lap dance."

The girl began smiling slightly. She inched her chair forward on the stage. The hypnotist moved off to the side.

Her body language was completely different from before. Whereas once she had been reserved and shy, an explainable reaction to someone suddenly called on stage, she was now loose and relaxed. She rose, walked up to her paying customer, and began swaying her hips back and forth with complete freedom. He watched as this beautiful girl looked into his eyes. He thought her lips were perfect. Her eyes were a calm brown, and her skin was Mediterranean. He was amazed at how striking she was.

He was also astonished at her willingness to suddenly give him a lap dance.

She placed her torso against him, while grinding his lap with fervent passion. The crowd gave a wild hoot, and his friends began yelling his name in support.

"Yea, dude! Jo-ey! Jo-ey!"

He couldn't help but let out a suppressed laugh. He was far more uncomfortable than she seemed to be. Despite the crowd's loud reaction, she continued to dance and grind to no sound in particular. At one point she turned around and let her bottom touch against his thighs.

He didn't understand what was happening *precisely*, but he wasn't about to interrupt the show with questions.

The hypnotist allowed this to happen a few minutes more until he snapped the girl from her seemingly trance-like state. She gave the impression that she hadn't even realized anything odd had happened. She had just tuned out everything else, seemed somewhat bewildered and confused, still waiting for something to happen. In a way for her, it *seemed* no different than being lost in a movie.

The crowd gave a wild round of applause. Both he and the girl climbed down off stage at the same time, her slightly confused expression was alluring with her palms upward, as if to ask, "Was *that* it?" She was ushered to her table where her friends welcomed her with a fit of laughter and hugs.

He watched her for a moment more but was soon greeted by his own friends and had to move on.

He would look over to her every so often throughout the rest of the show.

He made it a point to talk to her after the show, but the room was crowded, and it seemed like she had already gone.

Fear not, Glory Boy. Patience is a virtue.

It was another night out in Woodbridge. The late March air was frigid, and he was bundled up for warmth. His friends and he planned to go to a bar to unwind. It was a cool spot in Woodbridge that was popular with his crowd.

They walked into the building and were instantly greeted with the warmth of the bar.

His friends picked a place at the bar to sit when he noticed a girl with familiar brown eyes and hair in the crowd. He was pleasantly surprised to see the girl from the hypnotist's show a few weeks before. She and her friends from that night were standing around a table, enjoying a drink.

Without much thought, he walked over towards her with a smile. He couldn't believe his luck.

God, she is lovely...

"Hey there, aren't you the girl who gave me a lap dance last month?"

There had been better openers than that one. He had no way of fully knowing if she remembered him or not. He got his answer immediately.

"Excuse me?!" she said angrily. Her brown eyes were filled with fury.

"You gave me a lap dance at that hypnotist's show a month ago," he said.

I meant nothing rude by it.

"What the hell are you talking about?" she said.

He remembered her as more fun than *this*.

"No, he's right. You did," one of her friends said.

"That's right. You were hypnotized," another chimed in. *"We told you! You wouldn't believe us!"*

The girl looked between her friends dumbfounded, but she could *now* tell they weren't kidding. There was no joke, and he had not been in on it.

"Oh. Well, I'm sorry for being rude. I don't remember. I thought you were being a creep," the girl said, forcing herself to smile.

"No worries," he said, extending out a hand.

"We were never introduced on stage. My name's Joey."

She took his hand in hers.

She has soft skin, he thought.

There was something familiar to her touch, almost as if he had felt it before. Even with the lap dance, he had never actually touched her skin.

He couldn't place the feeling.

"Nice to meet you, Joey."

She told him her name.

They smiled at each other. Their eyes locked. Now there was only he and the girl, no disturbances or friends or noise.

The two broke apart their handshake and that first moment was gone.

"So, how old are you?" he asked her.

"Twenty," she replied. She took a sip of her drink, coyly hiding a smile.

"A year younger than me," he said.

Good start, carry on…

"So, what were you doing at that show anyway?"

"We thought it would be fun. We kind of like that stuff," The Girl said, speaking for her friends.

"What about you?"

"Oh, me and my friends love that place. We thought it would be fun to swing by," he said.

The Girl nodded.

"So, I take it you don't believe in that stuff?"

He laughed.

Ha! Of course not!

"Nah, I think it's kind of silly."

"Well, it got you a lap dance. It can't be too silly."

The Girl smiled at him.

He smiled back. He was beginning to like her.

"You got me there."

"Yo, Jo-ey!"

He turned around to see one of his friends waving at him from some seats at the bar. There was an empty one for him.

"I guess my friends are waiting for me. I'd hate to leave this conversation unfinished though. Would you want to swap numbers?"

There it was. The question had been asked. He wondered if it was too much, too soon.

She smiled. She reached into her purse and took out a blue pen and wrote her number down on a nearby napkin.

"Call me," she said, handing him her number.

"I *will* call you," he said.

"You'd better."

✧

Joey's first day working at the White Horse bar at Toronto Pearson was on September 11th, 2001.

Ah the astonishing art of timing.

There may have never been a worse day to start a job in history than this,
he thought.

And a job in an airport at that. There was that Japanese fellow
who survived the H-bomb in Hiroshima, only to escape to Nagasaki
to be hit again days later. Unlucky to be hit twice, but lucky to survive twice too?

Just like we all did, he walked into a new world that day; but his
a little more in-your-face. There were S.W.A.T. teams with machine
guns and assault rifles scattered all over, each of them on obviously
on high alert, and clearly not sure if an attack was coming to Toronto
as well.

He could only watch nervously, while cleaning glasses with a
white rag as police and security walked around with German shep-
herds and assault weapons.

The world had suddenly become a very weird place.

At least for him, his world had become a little better in recent
days. The Girl had helped him to get the job at the airport, allowing
him to quit his job at The Sports Club Bar.

She worked at a different bar in the other terminal. Time had
taken care of things between them. The two had started calling each
other after almost immediately after that night, and never stopped.
Eventually, probability swung in their favor, and before either of them
knew it, they were officially boyfriend and girlfriend. It had progressed over months of hanging out and enjoying weekends together.
It wasn't long before the two were allowed to sleep over each other's
houses, almost with no resistance from either side's parents. It wasn't
long before the two *were sleeping* together as well. The pair couldn't
ignore the attraction between them. It was impossible.

It was also impossible for him to stay faithful. He saw opportunities around him and didn't think twice.

When he had worked there for over a year, he just knew it was
time to leave. He quit.

He took one last look at the bar.

He then turned around and headed towards the airport's exit.

What on earth am I going to tell Mom and Dad?

✦

The same day, his friend L_____ gave him some good news over the phone.

"Dude, I know a place that needs people. It's easy work."

He was listening intently.

"What kind of work?" he asked.

"Vacation rentals. Like time-shares," L_____ said.

"What would I do?"

"You'd be a liner."

"What the hell's a *liner?*" he asked.

L_____ laughed.

"Someone that gets couples who want to go on vacation to speak with a salesman. It's like you're allowing the sales staff to close. You'd make easy money, man. Just like you were at the airport."

He couldn't say, "No."

"All right, man. I'll check it out. When can you introduce me?"

There was a brief pause.

"Today," L_____ replied.

✦

An hour later, the pair met up at a coffee house in Woodbridge. He got the low-down on the job, and then followed L_____ in his car to Travel, Inc.

The two parked outside the building and headed in together. L_____ introduced him to the boss and owner, Paul. He was tall, skinny, and balding. He spoke with a South Boston accent that could be confusing to follow. If he wanted a soda, he would always ask for a tonic. If someone actually did bring him tonic water, he would get mad. When he wanted a beer, he would pronounce it as, "Beeah," and if he wanted pizza he would say, "Pete Sir."

It could get a little confusing to understand him.

L_____ then scurried off, and then it was just Joey and the boss.

"All right, Joey. It's a simple job. Our marketing staff calls thousands of people a week. They send thousands of fliers every day. So, you don't have to worry about going to get people to come here. The only thing you have to worry about is getting these couples from the podium room to the salesroom. After that, we, the sales staff, take care of the rest. You go through a pamphlet with them over their free meal and talk them into a meeting with one of our guys. If you're good at it, you can move up to sales. You've got the potential to make at least two-fifty per couple if they sign up. That's cash, Joey. You think you can handle that?"

He took all of it in with stride.

"Yea, I think I can," he said.

The boss nodded.

"Good. Let me show you around."

He was a liner for only a month before being promoted.

He was thankful for that.

The conversations with the couples were often awkward, and he was getting tired of eating the same Chinese food every day. Chinese food was cheap though, and the couples were promised a meal. He just wished they would try pizza or tacos occasionally.

The podium room was a simple one with a power-point projector in front of several dozen seats. There were chairs lined up facing the lectern and a long table where the food was laid out buffet-style. A few tables in the back of the room allowed the couples to sit and eat their food while someone like Joey went over and joined them with his own plate. He perpetually carried a pamphlet with information listing the real prices of the vacation rentals that the presentation never mentioned. No one needed to be scared off. They needed to be lubricated with free food and smooth patter first.

"26,000? We're not paying that much just to go to Mexico!" they'd say.

"I totally understand. Neither would I. Let me have one of my managers talk to you before you go today," he would reply.

If they liked him, and many of them did, they would humor him and allow him to lead them into the salesroom. He would leave them in the capable hands of a colleague and swiftly return to his post in the podium room.

He had been personable enough with the couples, and lucky enough to have some of them close deals on vacations, that the boss, who had already taken a liking to his serious attitude and easy-going personality, promoted him.

"All right, Joey. Let me properly introduce you to the sales staff," the boss said to him in his office.

He was to start immediately.

The best teacher was experience.

The man in charge led him out onto the sales floor.

The team of eight was a ruthless picture of relentless patter and ambition at the pit-face of capitalism.

1: The Boss

Paul was at the top. He was the owner. The boss. The man with a plan.

He loved a single glass of very expensive Bordeaux – a *Pomerol '88* or *Saint Emilion '82* - when the moment demanded it, and astonishingly single-minded at work if sales were low. He believed in competition. Sometimes in the morning meetings, he would throw ten grand on the table and say, "Whoever gets the first sale of the day gets this cash."

He kept a board in the break room that showed everyone's numbers and sales. It bred rivalry. Like that Nat Geo documentary. He liked it like that. He wanted everyone to be wary of the other, always trying to one up the next person on the board.

He was in the business of making money and share in his success.

It's why he was excellent at being the boss. He had an authority about him that couldn't be denied. Nobody talked when he talked. Not even the best salesman in the room, 'Dr. Close'.

2: Ryan a.k.a. 'Dr. Close'

Ryan was a single-minded and loveable hustler from Germany. He had short blonde hair and blue eyes. He was so good at sales that he boasted often that he had written his own book about it called "Dr. Close". The 'book' was more of a pamphlet, but it was trusted so much that everyone in there had been forced to read it.

He would always put his glasses on before closing a sale and had the bizarre habit of always picking his teeth with something. It could be anything from a toothpick to a business card, but whatever it was, it would be somewhere lodged between his teeth. He even used his own bitten fingernails to floss his teeth.

Ryan also liked to gamble, and if his money wasn't being wasted on expensive brand clothing, it was being possibly being wasted on the craps tables at the casino. Rumor had it that he once lost thirty grand in one day, but Joey suspected this to be an exaggeration.

It was a good thing he was such a good closer at work.

3: Beirut Bill / Gargamel

Bill was from Lebanon and had a heavy accent. He was an amazing salesman, partly because people had to listen intently to what he was saying because his accent was so thick, his prey seemed mesmerized by the cadence and the entrancing cosine flow. He always wore a lot of jewelry, so when he wrote, almost everyone in the room could hear it clinging against the desk. He was a family man in his late forties. He had greyish hair and wore expensive-looking glasses.

Behind his back, the others referred to him as Gargamel, the hunched-over character from *The Smurfs*. He knew this, and, perversely, quite liked it, believing it an advantage in closing the deal.

4: Marco the Young Elvis

Marco was two years older than Joey, and the two were very close.

He was an electrician during the day and would boast of his conquests over lonely housewives, and even their friends over for innocent coffee and gossip. He was the only one allowed to come and go as he pleased, and because of this, and his slicked-back hair like a young Elvis Presley, was considered the cool one. He had worked there since he was a teenager and had developed an interesting quirk of sticking his hand out, leaning back, for someone to shake it without ever leaning in to meet the other halfway. The other person always felt obliged to move in and grab his hand. It was an opening power move that led to an astonishing sales record.

Of all the guys there, he was the most normal. Like the hot blonde in *The Munsters*, this made him stand out the most compared to the others.

Marco smelled like coconut-ty hair pomade and Sinatra's favorite body soap, *Agua Lavanda Puig*. The Young Elvis had done his homework.

5: Franco

Franco was a cheerful guy around forty with light hair. He was a big boy, and so incredibly animated that he persistently sweated like a squeezed teabag. He was known for using exaggerated hand gestures during his sales pitch with the clients, often saying, "Would you like a big package or a little package?" using his hands to rise to the level he was suggesting. If it were big package, his hands would go up past his head, and if it were a little package, they would go just above the table.

He was a storyteller, a superb raconteur. He loved to have the group of guys huddled around him to tell stories of past lovers, heartbreaks, and big sales he had landed in his youth. He was the bloke-at-the-end-of-the-bar, telling of the fish he'd reeled in, as the sweat rolled down his forehead and the damp patches on his shirt edged closer to each other.

6: Double H - a.k.a. Hungry Horace.

Horace was from Mexico and had a thick accent. He was Ryan's favorite, and, when he began to dress and walk like the German, the others considered him his Mexican *doppelgaenger*.

He wasn't the best salesman in the world, but when he did close, he wrote big numbers.

Horace had been a football agent, a record label guy, and Mexico City's coolest undercover cop. All the times he had to keep quiet about it in the past, well, he made up for it now, telling and re-telling his escapades, each time it seemed with a new dark twist.

7: Dmitri the Robot

Dmitri was Paul's right-hand man. He seemed to live only for the business. So much so that he was known for saying, "You can't miss work, even for a wedding." He was a remarkable salesman and a better closer. He was the most serious of them all, and robotic in his strive and ambition.

He was young too, a half-Croatian, half-Polish with black hair. He would always end his pitches with the open-ended question, "Visa, MasterCard or Amex?"

8: KGB Oscar.

Oscar was from Azerbaijan, and his eyes seemed to tell of a rough past there. They rarely blinked. The others could take one look into the man's eyes and know they had seen something terrible. No one gave him any nonsense.

They called him "KGB", because he talked his clients into submission. He ground it out of them, no matter how long it took. There would be times the others would want to leave, but they had to wait for Oscar to finish his pitch.

Nobody was allowed to leave until all the clients were gone.

In the end, though, the dark-haired man with eyebrows that resembled well-fed and errant, reclining slugs always got the sale.

After he had been introduced to everyone, Paul turned to him with a slight smile and said, "So, Joey Tomaselli, welcome to the Boiler Room."

Chapter 6

Set me free why don't cha babe
Get out my life why don't cha babe
'Cause you don't really love me
You just keep me hangin' on
(Holland, Dozier, Holland)

Some time, any time, between 2001 and 2008-

The Girl and he were sitting side by side on the plane, watching from their seats as his co-workers drank together from a few aisles up.

The boss sat next to Ryan, and they chatted about work over a nice Bordeaux he had brought along.

Franco was in the middle of a raunchy story that Joey could barely make out.

"And then she took the cherry pit out of the hole!"

The others erupted into laughter. Even Dmitri the Robot cracked a smile.

He knew he was frowning. He looked down at his hand. It was intertwined with The Girl's. He caught her looking at him, and so he smiled at her. She beamed back at him and gently squeezed his hand.

The group was going on holiday to Florida. They would check out their company's own resort - one of the ones they had been pushing on couples for years. It had been decided that a work holiday would be fun and motivational. And it was so far, for everyone except him, who felt split between his personal and professional worlds.

It was hard to say no to someone so beautiful.

And so, he suffered, as his co-workers had already started their vacation somewhere above Virginia.

"I can't wait to see Disney World," The Girl said.

"Yea, me too," he replied.

He looked out the window to his right. Puffy clouds floated harmlessly by the wing of the plane. They looked free and content to him.

He envied them, wishing it was just the two of them on the flight.

✧

The first few days of their weeklong trip had passed swiftly. Like always, his first instinct had been to grab some weed.

It was a chore for him, and his job alone, for she did not smoke.

And when his colleagues were slinging back shots at the club, he was sitting down to an expensive dinner with The Girl.

When they were gambling at the casino, he was walking around with The Girl.

When they were getting drunk and watching a mid-day movie and cracking jokes, he and The Girl were taking a nap.

Sometimes he wished he was with the men, but each morning he breathed a huge sigh of relief that he was not hungover.

They were all in the same time-share. They each had their own rooms, but it was like sharing a house. All he could hear from the others' rooms was loud rap music, and the sounds of laughter and drink glasses clinking together.

He didn't blame The Girl. She wasn't a party person. He loved her for that. She transcended all that, she was pure.

Joey however was flawed. The whole time she was nothing but

sweet, and did all she could to give him romance, but he was almost twenty-six and in his prime. He felt like he was missing out, and while the music played and the others bellowed out manly guffaws, he was sitting in bed at 10:45 p.m., The Girl next to him, reading a book.

The only things he liked to read were sports journals.

And he didn't feel much like reading.

"Are you having a good time, Joey?" The Girl asked several times.

"Of course, babe."

He kissed her on the cheek.

She kissed him back.

*There's no reason I can't have **any** fun.*

"'Fore!" Ryan yelled. The group watched the small white ball hit a nearby sand dune.

Dmitri nearly got hit and muttered something in his native tongue that the others were sure was a curse word of some kind.

The Girl and he were standing next to the golf cart, each hoping for the trip to end.

He wanted to get back to Toronto, so he could have free time again. The Girl wanted to get back because she was tired of hanging around with this team.

"Shit," Ryan said. He walked over to the dune to try to get his ball out.

It was the last day in Florida, and Joey had enjoyed very little of it. He felt like a dog being brought to the park only to be tied up on a leash, while free canines pissed on trees and larked with rapturous and euphoric abandon.

"You're never going to finish this round," Franco said. The others snickered at Ryan's expense.

He looked over at The Girl. She looked good in her summer shorts and crop top. A slight breeze caught her almond hair. There was a delicate smile on her face, carefree. The wind carried the smell of her conditioner to his nostrils. It reminded him of something sweet.

She looked perfect. She smelled perfect. She rarely argued, and she was always polite. This all underlined that Joey perhaps could never be happy.

So why am I not happy?

"There, I got it, ya bunch of clowns," Ryan said, his ball making it back onto the green a few yards from the sixteenth hole.

"You're up, Joey," The Boss said from behind a beer can.

"Sounds good," he replied.

Sounds good.

✿

Jamaica was hot.

Sure, he and The Girl kind of knew that already, but they had no idea *how* hot it would be.

By the time they had left the airport and made it to the bus that would take them to the resort, they were already drenched in sweat.

"I hope the bus has air conditioning," The Girl said. She was fanning her face with a brochure.

"Me too," he said.

More than that though, he was, of course, hoping to score some weed. He figured the birthplace of Bob Marley must have something potent and reasonably accessible.

The two gave their suitcases to one of the attendants who lobbed them into an undercarriage. The Girl and he then got onto the bus.

The two had to wait another twenty minutes for the vehicle to get going. When it finally did, nearly fifty sweaty people were packed into it, each seemingly groaning and mumbling about something.

At least when the bus started, the A.C. worked.

"Hello, everyone. Thank you for choosing to stay with Paradise Jamaican Resorts. We should be arriving at our beautiful beach location in about two hours."

Immediately, there was a series of loud sighs.

"But" the attendant continued, "there will be a short stop for drinks along the way. We appreciate your patience, and once again, thank you for choosing your vacation with Paradise Jamaican Resorts."

The intercom turned off with a crackle, and he thought to himself, "Fine. I'll get it when we stop for drinks."

✿

Forty-five minutes later, the bus pulled off into a small town. Street dogs roamed around freely, and some kids played basketball nearby, using a soccer ball for the game.

Five minutes after that, he was in a narrow-ish pathway at the side of a close-by gas station trying to buy some weed. He shifted around nervously as he handed two men some cash.

They had asked for forty, but he knew that for what he was getting, it would have cost twenty-five back home.

But he couldn't argue. It wasn't his turf.

The two men left to go get the weed, and for a second he felt stupid. He knew they could have just taken his money and left.

But five minutes later they came back with the goods and the deal was done.

He walked back to the bus, happy with his weed, while she was wondering where he had gone. It hadn't been the first trip he had slipped off to procure drugs from some shady corner. It had happened in Aruba, it had happened in Cancun, and it had happened in Miami.

But what could he do?

He needed it.

✿

At the resort, he wanted more.

He would tip the bussers extra at the restaurants to bring him back weed after their shift. Sometimes he would find a bellhop and tip him instead. Whoever it was, he was giving some eager and hip cat money for drugs for each of the seven days they were there.

Sure, they snorkeled in the water in the morning, held hands at dinner, and walked along the beaches in the evening but come mid-morning, mid-afternoon and nighttime, he would always find himself alone outside, smoking a joint and watching the waves crash onto the sand.

Sometimes when he was standing there alone, he would catch the glimpse of a female looking over at him. She might be walking along the beach by herself and she would smile at him. He would smile back and while nothing ever happened, it stirred something inside of him.

Something primordial.

And he liked it.

And because he liked it, he couldn't help but ask himself once more,

Why am I not happy?

He would always then look down at his joint for the answer, but all that it gave him was a euphoric buzz and red eyes.

"It's been over five years already, Joey. When are we going to get married?"

She looked into his eyes, hoping for a different answer than the last seven times.

His gaze shifted away from her.

"That's why we're getting the condo. It's just not ready yet," he said.

The condo was a two-year investment for him. In two different ways, the first, was that since he worked a mostly commission-based job, his last two years' worth of income had to be approved just to be considered, and the second was that they were new condominiums along The Queensway. They took two years to build. The idea was to move in together when it was ready.

She tried finding some deeper truth behind his irises but couldn't find anything.

So, like always, she dropped it.

For now.

The two were lying in bed, snuggling. The travel channel played on the TV. It was an episode about the perks of traveling alone.

He turned the volume up.

☼

They had a home-cooked meal with Mary and Silvio. After dinner, he went to his room, and she went home to her place. He, despite the money he made working at the boiler room, was still living with his parents. It allowed him to save a lot of money, and he was going to need it for the condo.

While he was lying on his bed contemplating marriage, he noticed his jacket hanging from his chair. He remembered something he had left inside the pocket.

Het got up from his spot on the bed and grabbed it. He reached his hand inside it and retrieved a slip of paper with a number on it. Above the number was the name "Rachel." He remembered her from a party a week ago.

He thought about it. Then he took out his cell phone and typed in the number on the slip of paper.

Hey Rachel, this is Joey from the party. How have you been? I was wondering if you wanted to...

☼

A couple months later, he had been relaxing at home, drinking a can of soda when he got the call from The Girl.

"Hey, honey. I'm looking at this beautiful banquet hall downtown. I want to put a deposit down. It's so gorgeous."

He nearly spat the drink.

The hunter had become the hunted. He had always been the one to get the deals closed at work. There was rarely a couple he couldn't coerce with his charms into some expensive packaged deal. He was the one who dictated the rules of engagement, and he, like the mighty lion of the African savannah, was the one to eat first. However, the game had suddenly been played backwards, and it was now he who was the prey.

"What do you mean, you're looking at halls?"

"I'm downtown looking at wedding halls for us. I've been looking at them all day, but I finally found a good one."

"I haven't asked you to marry me yet though," he said, straightening up in his chair. "Why would you be looking for a wedding hall without an engagement ring?"

"Oh, I was just checking them out for us in advance," she replied. He could tell from the tone of her voice she thought she had done nothing odd.

"Okay, well, don't put any money down. I haven't asked you yet. Okay?"

There was a sigh on the other end of the phone, but she eventually gave a reluctant, "Okay."

"All right. Thanks. We'll talk later," he said.

"Okay."

A pause.

"Love you."

But he had already hung up.

He was already thinking about what that conversation meant for the future of their relationship.

Damn, he thought, putting his drink down on the table.

I gotta do something about this.

"So, then it turned out he was the one wearing the horse mask!"

Joey and the others burst out laughing. It had been another great story from Franco.

Everyone, except Dmitri and The Boss, was huddled around Franco's desk, exchanging stories until the next round of couples came through. It had been just another day in the boiler room.

Then, the door to the main office opened and out walked The

Boss. He had a grim look on his face. His lips were still and impassive, his expression like a mask.

"Everyone, I got some bad news. Listen up," Paul said.

Dmitri seemed to appear from nowhere and took a seat with the others.

"So, the news is this: A new law is about to pass in a few weeks. Basically, the couples we are selling packages to will now have a ten-day cooling-off period after buying. This means that they have up to ten days to cancel with us legally and get a full refund. I have to be honest. This is going to hurt and possibly kill us."

The smiles had faded. The horse mask story was forgotten. Even the robotic Dmitri seemed to show a hint of worry and looming trouble.

"So, what's the plan?" Ryan asked.

"Well, we'll give it some time. Five months, maybe six. We'll see how it goes."

Joey shifted in his chair uncomfortably. He felt change fast approaching him, though it was just a gut thing. If he were asked at the time, he wouldn't have been able to put it into words. It felt the same as that sometimes strange and unexplainable energy that connects everyone and everything together during tragic moments in life, like a hurricane or earthquake. It was there again at that moment, and for that time, they were no longer competing with each other.

There was no rivalry.

There were just some men in a room, uncertain of the future.

Six months later, change had indeed come. It was strong enough to upset the entire business model, and it wasn't long before the money stopped coming in. The ten-day cooling period turned out to be perhaps the one thing that could end the business.

Couples naturally began to say to themselves the day after buying some expensive package, "Oh, I think I was hasty!" and they'd call back and cancel. And there was nothing any of them could do about it.

Not even Joey's charm, nor anyone else's, could do a damn thing.

It wasn't long before he knew he had to quit. The others were already quitting too.

Beirut Bill went to go sell used cars. KGB Oscar went to go work at a laundromat. Ryan moved to the States. Dmitri the Robot became a butcher, his family's business. Who knows where Franco went. Hungry Horace became a busser downtown at a taco shop. Marco continued working as an electrician. The Boss, well, he had turned out okay. It was his business after all. He took what he could and moved back to Boston.

Joey got a job selling phones downtown at Bell.

He had felt the era coming to a close six months prior and now it finally had.

He said goodbye to them all in person before he left. Seven years was a long time to be surrounded by the same group of people.

But like everything in life, the cycle had come to its natural conclusion.

Over.

Sayonara.

Finito.

The boiler room had bubbled over.

He would never see any of them again. He was proud of his time and achievements there.

A few days later, he was driving around town and thought he would call her. He held his cell phone up to his ear and heard her voice on the other end of the line.

"I'm with friends," she said. He could hear the unmistakeable noise of a bar in the background. The sound of pool balls clacked in the distance and music played.

"You swear to God?" he asked. He knew she was religious. It was like asking someone to swear on their mother's life. He wasn't sure why he was acting jealously. It wasn't like him, but he still felt like something was wrong. Really, he just needed an excuse. The change had not been felt only at his job. This had been a long time coming.

"I swear to God," she said.

He pulled up to where she was. He saw her through the front window of the building sitting with two men from her work where she worked as an assistant for an investment group.

"Then how come I can see you sitting with two guys right now?" he said.

She looked up from her place at the table and made eye contact with him, who was parked in front of the bar.

She was speechless.

"Yea, we're done," he said.

He hung up the phone, put the car in reverse, and drove off down the street.

For the first time in their seven-year relationship, he felt free.

"Thanks for moving in with me, man, you're really helping me out with the rent, even if it is just short-term" he said to his friend, Anthony, who was just finishing putting the last of his boxes into his new room.

"No problem, man. I know this is a weird time for you. And you were supposed to be in your new place with her. Funny how I end up moving in with you on the first day."

"Yea, life can be odd," he replied.

The break-up hadn't been funny though. She had tried calling him over and over again, each time trying new ways to apologize for what had happened, but he never budged. Not even for a passionate night.

Even her mom tried calling him a couple times to describe the state of depression her daughter was in. She told him she would catch her crying on her bedroom floor.

It wasn't that he liked seeing her in pain. He loved her. She did nothing wrong really. She had told him they were just guys from work, and he knew he had no right to complain.

He remembered Rachel.

And Sophia. And Lucy. And Melanie.

She was excused for her actions. She was perfect.

Just not for him.

"That's the last of it, right?" he asked Anthony.

Anthony nodded. "Yep. So, what do you want to do now?"

He thought for a moment.

"Let's get some weed," he said to himself.

Depression is a mood disorder that causes a persistent feeling of sadness and loss of interest. Also called major depressive disorder or clinical depression, it affects how you feel, think and behave and can lead to a variety of emotional and physical problems. You may have trouble doing normal day-to-day activities, and sometimes you may feel as if life isn't worth living.

More than just a bout of the blues, depression isn't a weakness and you can't simply "snap out" of it. Depression may require long-term treatment. But don't get discouraged. Most people with depression feel better with medication, psychotherapy or both.

—Mayo Clinic

Chapter 7

From May 2008 to March of 2009, life was a blur.

And now he was in Las Vegas with his pals, replicating his Toronto existence in the desert.

There were things about Vegas that would end up defining the short life and times of Joey Tomaselli. The city was a kind of barometer of his dreams and demons. It was almost as if he could make it there, he could make it anywhere. It was his white whale, his *Moby Dick*. The desert is full of mirages. And therefore, it dashed hopes. But sometimes mirages are reality, and Vegas has crowned many a World Champion and made many a millionaire. But for everyone boxer with a belt and a gambler with a sack of hundreds, there are a thousand poor and condemned souls walking the streets, head down, just looking for a place to end it.

As I walk this land with broken dreams
I have visions of many things

> But happiness is just an illusion
> Filled with sadness and confusion.
> > (What Becomes of the Broken-
> > Hearted - Jimmy Ruffin)

Vegas was vile that day. Moms with strollers lurched down the sidewalk. Men handed out cards advertising strip clubs and escort services to strangers. Quaint churches sat snugly next to twenty-four-hour bars. The homeless slept where the rich walked. It stank. To him, the entire city was a façade; a big, fat, phony façade.

Savi, Anthony, AJ and he didn't care though. They weren't there to philosophize or scrutinize the city. They were there to have fun. His whole year had been like this. None of them knew about his drug use.

Months had passed since the break-up and the move in with Anthony. It had been good for his freedom, bad for his health. There was hardly a day that passed where he wasn't out having fun.

The women too had been as constant as the booze, and almost as potent. Minor relationships that lasted no more than two weeks scattered his calendar days throughout the months since he had left The Girl.

She hadn't taken it well and had often shown up at his condo with her friends or at the club where he was hanging out. She had even rebounded with some guy during the process, yet it never stopped her from trying to rekindle the relationship.

She was persistent. He would give her that.

He was lucky to have Anthony, who was the barrier to any possible meeting.

It worked for a while, but, at some point, he knew he had to face her.

She had only ended up leaving him alone once he told her he had cheated on her. From then on, there had been silence, and he assumed the healing process could now begin. He missed her, and the affection she had brought into his life. For a while, he couldn't watch romantic movies with his temporary girlfriends, because they reminded him of

The Girl. He'd tell the *dame-du-jour* to turn off whatever sappy movie they were watching.

They reminded him too much of **her.**

All he could face was alcohol, drugs, women, and his friends.

They were walking down the street.

"Hey, let's go in here," Savi said.

He took a look at the flashy sign in front of the club that read, "Thursday special: Five dollar drinks."

Nice, he thought.

"All right, let's do it," he replied.

Savi smiled. The others were excited as well. It was their first day of their four-day trip, and they couldn't think of a better way to start it off. He couldn't either. He could never have done this before when he was in a relationship. This was the freedom he had wanted so badly. Finally, he was in the middle of it, enjoying every moment.

He hoped the feeling would last forever. He was going to ride the rollercoaster, like that crazy one in the lobby of the Paris hotel on the strip. He smiled.

But…

February 2009-

The sink was full of cold water, and he splashed his face in it.

The weed had stopped working like it was supposed to. It no longer made him feel good, and the highs were coming with extreme lows that made him feel paranoid and anxious. Instead of nudging him into a groove, it was making him feel edgy and odd.

I feel different.

He wasn't sure why it wasn't as effective. It felt like it might be harming him, but he couldn't just stop. Weed was all he knew as a cure. It was *his* medicine. He didn't have any other kind.

He brought his head up from the water and examined himself in the mirror. His skin was paler than usual, and his eyelids seemed droopy. The reflection in the mirror no longer seemed to resemble the person he had known all his life. He knew it was the same old weed as always, and so therefore the laws of common sense would mean the change must be inside him.

What the hell am I supposed to do?

The thought swam around inside his head for a few seconds.

No answer came.

✧

April 16ᵗʰ, 2009 - 10:00 pm -

He was supposed to be promoting a night at the Century Room nightclub with his friend, Niels. Niels was a tall Dutchman with light brown hair and a cheeky smile that seemed to suggest he knew more than he was letting on. His passion was swimming, and this accentuated his lean, athletic frame. Like his pal, Niels relished the club scene.

They had met months prior at the Century Room. A friend-in-common had introduced the two of them and they had hit it off instantly. It had been perfect timing too, as Anthony had met a girl, who was moving into the other place. He needed a new place to stay, and Niels' apartment seemed to provide the solution to a long-held dream; to live in a high rise downtown. He had always wanted to be able to see the whole city and look down on it like a king in his castle. Niels offered to share the place, and so in early April the two signed a lease together.

It was now his first night in the apartment, and his first time promoting for his friend at the club. God, this should have been a brave new world for him, everything was coalescing, coming together. Yet something didn't feel right.

There was a snag.

He felt like shit.

He sent Niels a text to let him know.

I feel like shit bro

Maybe I need to smoke some more, he thought.

He was in the bathroom, washing his face for the third time that night. The intended highs still weren't accomplishing anything. He only ever felt sick.

He turned off the lights and headed into his bedroom. He had purposely avoided choosing the other bedroom with the balcony and had yet to even step out on the patio attached to the living room. They were on the forty-fourth floor of the building, and though he had never been particularly afraid of his heights, he *now* dreaded being up that high. He didn't know for sure, if it was because of how the weed had been making him feel since the winter or if his long-held dream had become a nightmare over-night. Now it didn't matter if he could see Lake Ontario from the window. He felt nauseous.

He grabbed some more weed from his drawer and placed the bag on the bed. He turned on the TV and flipped through the channels until he came to *The Score*. They were playing NBA highlights, but he wanted to see the hockey.

He felt truly awful.

11:54 pm-

He took another hit of weed. It was what he always did to feel better. It was an engrained response to any kind of emotional dip.

The smoke billowed out of his mouth towards the window. The city was lit up in all its fluorescent charm and bold glory.

He was lying down on his bed, trying to relax. Finally, the hockey highlights played on the TV. The Maple Leafs were getting thrashed by the Devils. The score was five to zero.

He sighed.

Will the Leafs ever win?

Usually, he would shrug and think of girls. But even the thought of the Leafs messing up made him give a little twitch.

What was that? What the hell was that, Joey?

Then, his eye flickered. His neck and chin spasmed, a small but steady and definite shock sent down his spine. His temples felt hot, and

a muscle in his left thigh flickered once, twice until he was forced to sit down. His left elbow darted up, as if he were chasing off a housefly.

Oh Christ!

11:55 pm-

A jolt of sickness made its way up his oesophagus. He thought he was going to puke. This weed continued to give none of the familiar and euphoric high he had known for most of his life. It was something different. He felt wretched again. Whatever it was, it was coming in powerful waves of nausea.

He smelled the weed. It stank the same as always.

It's me. The problem is me. The problem is YOU, Joey. You've used up all your lives. It is time to pay. No more free rides, man.

He sat up. He felt the room around him begin to shift. Was that an earthquake?

Don't blame the earthquake. You wish it were an earthquake. That would be too easy. Life is not that easy. It is you that is a mess, Joey Tomaselli.

His breathing started to pick up, accompanied by a definite tightness in his chest.

What the hell is going on right now? What's happening?

He tried to stand up but stumbled. He placed a hand on the wall to steady himself.

Oh shit. This isn't good. I am done for.

The voice of the hockey commentator seemed to taunt him.

Another crushing defeat. There's no coming back from this.

It then morphed back into his own voice.

Defeat.

11:56-11:57 pm-

What the hell is wrong with me?

A warm rush of adrenaline surged through his body, as he puked on his feet. The rising stink made him wretch and vomit again, as spittle trailed down onto his torso.

Why is the room spinning? Everything is twisting and swirling around. I need something to eat. I need something to eat. I need something to eat...

The thoughts of food took him to the kitchen, where he grabbed a bowl from the cabinet. He shakily opened up the fridge door and grabbed the milk. He took the box of Vector cereal from the counter and dumped some into the bowl.

Sugar will level me out.

Time seemed to stop. Everything slowed down as his mind raced.

Am I even here right now? What the hell is going on? Am I going to be okay? Is this going to be over soon? Will this cereal help? I guess I should eat it. I guess I should eat it.

He grabbed a spoon from the drawer, slammed it into his cereal, and began eating greedily. He shoveled it in.

It didn't work.

The taste of the cereal on an *amuse-bouche* of barf made him feel sick once again, so he dropped the bowl, and reeled towards the sanctuary of the couch, spitting out remnants, his hands clawing at his face.

11:58- 11:59 pm-

The building is still moving, man. The building is going to crumble. I got to get out of here. I have to go home.

He grabbed his car keys from the countertop. He took out his phone from his pocket and tried to message Niels with wobbly thumbs that stunk of puke. Each error in typing hacked away at his tenuous spirit.

Think im having panic attack go ing to my pare nts

He walked to the front door, grabbed his shoes from the mat, and slipped them on. Little beads of sweat dropped from his forehead onto the floor.

His cell phone buzzed in his hand.

Dude, are you serious? I have two girls ready to come over. Just hold up.

I have to leave. I have to go, Niels.

I cant

He hit the 'send' button on the phone and put it back in his pocket.

I have to get back home.

12:00 am-

He exited the apartment and locked the door behind him. The hall-way seemed to be unending. He began walking towards the elevators, but with each step he took, they seemed to get farther away.

Jesus. What is this?

A couple letting themselves in to an apartment scowled and frowned at him. They were with one other girl, who may have appeared concerned. He tried to avoid eye contact.

I know what you're thinking. But I am not high on crystal or coke. I am not buzzing out. I'm not a fricking crack head. I had a bad spliff. I am sick. I need help. Please don't look at me.

He held his breath. He was so tense. He was forgetting to breathe. He needed oxygen.

I can hear my pulse in my neck. Why can I hear a pulse in my neck?

Ba-doom! Ba-doom! Ba-doom! Ka-boom! Ka-boom! Ka-boom!

The thumping from his neck vein resonated on his ear drum. There were two distinct pitches. A ba-doom and a ka-boom.

He reached the elevators, after what seemed like several minutes. He pressed the down button on the panel and prayed the elevator would come quickly. He felt the walls closing in.

This whole damned place is going to come down. I just know it. I know it will. I knew I should not have moved in here. How do these people live like this?

Ba-doom! Ba-doom! Ba-doom!

"Moooothhhhhhheeerrrr! My neck!"

Ba-doom! Ba-doom! Ba-doom!

12:01 am -

The elevators came to a stop. When the doors opened, he gladly stepped inside. He pressed the button over, and over again until the doors closed. It began its descent towards the underground car park.

Ba-doom! Ba-doom! Ba-doom!

Please, no-one come in here. Please, I pray.

This whole place is going to come apart. Everything here is about to break. The building is about to collapse. I have to get out of here. Please get me out of here.

Ba-doom! Ba-doom! Ba-doom! Ka-boom!

The elevators seemed to move inch by inch as he leaned his back against the wall for support. He puked again but weakly, just putrid and acidic gut juice and a couple of pieces of masticated cereal. He wiped his face with his forearm and saw in the metal mirrored interior his reflection and pupils like saucers.

Pins and needles in my arm. In my left arm. I'm having a heart attack.

He was still breathing short, raspy breaths, and the buzzing energy still circulated within him.

Please, someone help me. My neck is throbbing, it's going to explode.

Ba-doom! Ba-doom! Ba-doom! Ka-boom!

Ba-doom! Ba-doom! Ba-doom! Ka-boom!

Ba-doom! Ba-doom! Ba-doom! Ka-boom!

Mama, you will help me. You're the only one. I'm coming to you.

12:02-12:03 am-

His visceral reaction to seek his mother's embrace was that of a soldier in a foxhole. There were doctors within easy reach, he could dial 911, but logic was absent. He did not consider medical help. He did not want to be stopped by the police in this state. He wanted Mary, even if it meant getting behind the wheel of a car and driving many miles to her. He did not even consider a taxi. He had passed the point of cogent thought, poor boy. Still with the pulse in his neck....

Ba-doom! Ba-doom! Ba-doom! Ka-boom!

Ba-doom! Ba-doom! Ba-doom! Ka-boom!

Ba-doom! Ba-doom! Ba-doom! Ka-boom!

The elevator doors opened on the ground floor, and he stumbled towards his car a few yards away.

He pressed the button on the key chain and unlocked the vehicle.

He got in and closed the door behind him.

Jesus, I can barely breathe. I have to get out of here before the building collapses. I don't want to be buried down here. Breathe, Joey. Just breathe.

He put the keys into the ignition, checked his disturbing mien in the mirror, shook his head as if that would help, and started the car.

Ok, let's go!
Ba-doom! Ba-doom! Ba-doom! Ka-boom!

12:04 am-

He reversed out of the parking spot, then put the car in drive, and sped off to the ramp and into the neon-lit horror show of the city at night outside.

I have to get out of here. I have to get out of here. I have to get out...
Ba-doom! Ba-doom! Ba-doom! Ka-boom!

Trails of red and silver car lights flashed by slowly and quickly, as if he were in some virtual reality, high intensity video game. Horns sounded at bizarre pitches. There were flashes of light around his field of vision, and one eye felt a viscous layer that blurred the road ahead. He slowed down, pulled over. He breathed deeply. And then took off at high speed again.

Moootthhhheeerrrrr!!!!
Ba-doom! Ba-doom! Ba-doom! Ka-boom!

The sound of his pulse now thumped in both ears, and he could feel it vibrate in his neck more powerfully than ever. He opened a window and stuck his head out like a Labrador on a warm day.

"Crazy asssssssssshhhhollllllle!" came the cry from a vehicle.
Ba-doom! Ba-doom! Ba-doom! Ka-boom!

12:05 am-

He was on the road, heading for his parents' house.

I think I'm going the right way. I don't know.

He needed help, so he did the only thing he knew how.

He began to pray.

Please get me home, God. I promise to be a good boy, if You let me see my mama.

Ba-doom! Ba-doom! Ba-doom! Ka-boom!
Oh no. God won't listen to a jerk like me.

12:06 am-

"Uncle Robert, it's me, Joey. I know you're not here anymore, and I don't talk to you as much as I should, but I could really use your help right now. I don't know what the hell is going on with me. I don't feel good, and everything is spinning. My whole body feels off. I don't get it, Uncle Robert, I really don't. Please, if you're listening to me, I could really use your help right now. I'm scared."

Ba-doom! Ba-doom! Ba-doom! Ka-boom!

12:07 am-

He was on the highway and driving as fast as he could.

Despite his foot being hard down on the pedal, it still felt as if the car was only going forty kilometers per hour.

I don't know if I'm going to make it...

A cop car's blue lights flashed, and the siren blurred and then disappeared in the opposite direction.

Did something just go right for me? You're using up your lives, Joey. I reckon that was your ninth life. Next time, it is time's up for you.

12:08- 12:26 am-

He had been on the highway for nearly twenty minutes before exiting. It felt like it was the right one.

I might be wrong. I don't know.

To him, it felt like it had been two hours.

Once off the ramp, a red light forced him to come to a halt.

He stared at the neon rouge, trying to will it to change to green.

It stayed the same, as if to taunt him.

Change. Please Change!

Ba-doom! Ba-doom! Ba-doom! Ka-boom!

Ba-doom! Ba-doom! Ba-doom! Ka-boom!

Ba-doom! Ba-doom! Ba-doom! Ka-boom!

Ba-doom! Ba-doom! Ba-doom! Ka-boom!

His car was the only one on that road, and still the light remained red and unaffected by his wishes. It didn't care he was suffering or that he could barely think straight.

He was beginning to get desperate. His parents' house was just over ten minutes away.

He was so close to safety.

Am I close to safety?

He needed to see his mom.

"I'll never smoke another joint again. No more weed. No more cigarettes. I promise. Just please, let me get home!"

He could feel tears well up behind his eyes.

"Please, Uncle Robert. Get me home safely."

The light changed to green.

He sighed in relief.

He pressed his foot back down on the pedal and peeled off, leaving the past and the smoke behind him.

Ba-doom! Ba-doom! Ba-doom! Ka-boom!

Ba-doom! Ba-doom! ...

He was outside the house. He was an absolute mess. He looked like he had been on a week-long jag.

Oh Jesus, Dad is going to kill me. I have to explain I am sick. Uncle Robert, one more favour, please.

Ba-doom! Ba-doom! Ka-boom!

Ba-doom! Ka-boom! Ka-boom! Ka-boom!

Ba-doom! Ka-boom! Ka-boom! Ka-boom!

PART THREE

Panic disorder refers to recurrent, unexpected panic attacks (e.g., heart palpitations, sweating, trembling) followed by at least one month of:

- constant concern about having another panic attack or the consequences of a panic attack (e.g., having a heart attack), and/or
- significant behaviour changes related to the attacks (e.g., avoiding exercise or places for fear of having a panic attack).

A panic attack is a sudden feeling of intense fear or discomfort that peaks within minutes. It includes stressful physical and cognitive symptoms as well as behavioural signs.

—CAMH Toronto

t was nearly one a.m. when he arrived at his childhood home in suburban Brampton. There was an eerie stillness to the night that often accompanied such late times in the outskirts of Toronto. How odd that one could feel incredibly alone and afraid in the suburbs and yet in the city, surrounded by weirdos, murderers, and cretins, one would easily feel at peace. But not him. Not tonight.

Still buzzing sideways from his panic attack, he felt this uncomfortable silence as he left his car and made his way towards the side door of his parents' house. He had his own key and was able to let himself in. When he turned the handle to the door, he was met with the same childhood smells that he remembered. Marinara sauce, apple pie, his mother's perfume. It didn't make him feel welcome though. Rather, it gave him the sense that he was somewhere he didn't belong. He had already grown up and left, and now, at nearly twenty-nine, he was returning home, a failure. He knew he was never going back to that apartment in the city.

The only ones left inside the home were his parents. The two often slept in separate rooms as Silvio tended to snore heavily. Mary would be in a spare bedroom, either asleep or watching TV. Not that it mattered to her son what she was doing, he just needed to see her.

He needed help.

He walked past the kitchen and headed towards his mother's room. He knocked on the door as quietly as he could without it being totally inaudible.

"Mom?" he said into the darkness.

The sound of a small grunt, accompanied by shuffling and footsteps, could be heard on the other side of the door. A light flicked on, illuminating the space where his feet were planted. Then, the door opened, and he could now see just how bad he looked from the shocked look in his mother's eyes.

"Joey…," Mary's voice trailed off as she looked over her disheveled son. He could see the look of concern spread over his mother's face. Her eyes welled up.

I'm so sorry, Mom. I don't know what is wrong with me, please help me.

"What's wrong?"

He was still covered in sweat and feeling nauseous. He smelled like vomit, and his eyes were bloodshot. His hands trembled slightly, and inside of him, that buzzing energy coursed continuously.

He felt he couldn't answer.

"I think you had a panic attack, *amore*."

This made it worse for him. He was either having one, or had had one, but it was the concern and worry in Mary's voice that made him feel even more afraid.

God Just how bad do I look right now? Get a hold of yourself, man. Get a hold...

He cleared his throat before finally speaking.

"Yea, Mom. I think I must be. I don't know what's going on with me. I needed to come home."

He felt like crying.

"Come here."

Mary embraced her son and held him in the doorway.

Don't cry, Joey. Don't cry.

"Let's get you something to help you sleep, okay?" Mary said.

He nodded solemnly, and the two left each other's warm embrace.

They walked to the kitchen together. Mary flicked on the light and opened up a cabinet. While she rifled through it, he stood awkwardly, unsure of what to do with himself.

What am I going to do? Nobody's even here anymore. Nadia's gone. Sandra's gone. It's just me, he thought.

"Here we go. Melatonin. This will help," Mary said, taking a small bottle from the cabinet.

She opened it up, took two tablets out and placed them in his hand. She then grabbed a clean glass and filled it halfway with water, and then handed it to him. He took the pills and washed them down.

"That should help you sleep."

"Thanks, Mom."

He already knew he would need something more than melatonin. The buzzing inside of him was a clear reminder.

"I have to call the doctor in the morning, Mom. This is too much. I feel so much pain and anxiety right now."

"My God, Joey. What did you take?"

No point in hiding it anymore.

"Just weed, Mom. Just weed. I don't know why this happened."

He was beginning to shake with fear.

Mary walked over to her son and placed a gentle hand on his shoulder.

"It's okay, Joey. It's okay. Why don't you go to your room for now? Get some sleep. We can call the doctor tomorrow first thing in the morning when they open. Your father has work in six hours. Let's not wake him."

He nodded, unable to give a full reply. He was just too messed up.

The two said goodnight and he walked towards the same room he had slept in for so many years. The same place where he had been unable to write journals as a kid. Everything about it, no matter how he toyed with it inside his mind, was like heading backwards. Regression. Failure. Incompetence. Sadness.

Back to the place where it all began. He just never thought he would be back like this.

The pills were weak. Two would not cut it. His body fought them and easily won. He had done nothing but toss and turn since one-forty-five. He tried staying completely still, as if he were a plank of wood, but it only took five minutes for the restlessness to begin once more. He tried to sleep but then realised he was tense, he needed to let go again. There was nothing he could do to fall asleep. All he could do was think. In a sad and lonely loop. Reminders of failure.

Why is this happening to me? What am I going to do? Is it because of **her**? *Is this karma for hurting her? For cheating on her? Is this because of everything I did over the last ten years? What the hell did I do to deserve this shit? What am I supposed to do now? I can't go back. I know I can't. I'm sorry Niels, but I can't.*

-I hurt.

-I can't believe you paid 1,900 dollars just to stay in a place for one night. First and last month's rent my ass. Pathetic!

Shut up! I just need to think.... I just need to think. No. I need to sleep. Please, God, please! Let me just sleep!

His wishes were granted around five a.m.

⛣

He woke at just past seven in the morning. He had lain purposely still after he roused, so he wouldn't run into his father. He waited for Silvio to leave for the shop before allowing himself to get up from his bed. He knew he would have to face him eventually, but he wasn't ready just yet.

He headed downstairs to the basement at a quarter past seven. There was nothing he could do until the doctor's office opened, so he walked around there for nearly two hours, lost in thought.

I can't go back. My life is never going to be the same anymore. Not after last night. I guess that was a panic attack. It doesn't make any sense. Am I being punished? Did I really do something horrible? Is it really because of The Girl? Should I apologize to her? Who do I need to apologize to for this to go away? Jesus, why can't I have any answers. What the hell am I even doing down here? What time is it? Let me check my phone. Jesus, only seven forty-eight.

His thoughts continued to circle inside his head just as he himself circled the basement. Both his mind and legs were stuck in a loop like a caged and mentally diminished beast, and nothing could break the pattern, except for time.

There isn't anything to go back to now. I can't go back. My life has changed. Whose fault is this? What did I do wrong? What time is it?

Nine minutes had passed.

I can't go back to Niels. My life there is over. What did I do wrong? What time is it? He re-played old soccer games in his head to remember better times. He thought of good days, fun nights. He thought of his friends, and his family. He tried to tell himself to think of something nice, but each time he would land on a vicious reminder of something shitty.

Three minutes had passed.

I can't go back there. My life is never going to be the same. What the hell is wrong with me? What time is it? What time is it? What time is it?

⛣

Finally, nine o'clock came around, and he struggled his way back upstairs and into the kitchen. Mary was waiting for him, a cup of tea in her hand.

"Here you go, *amore*. Drink."

"Later, Mom. Let's call first," he said, ignoring the hot cup.

He picked up the house phone and keyed in the number to the doctor's office.

The clock on the wall read 9:02. He hoped there would be no wait.

"Good morning, thank you for calling Brampton Health. My name is Jennifer, how may I help you?"

The woman's voice was cheery and bright and was completely lost on him.

"Hi. This is Joey Tomaselli. I need to see Dr. Brian right away."

His tone was rushed and pleading. There was no time for formalities or politeness.

I need something. Anything.

"Okay, well, let me just check the computer to see if he has any open slots. Give me one moment, please."

"Thank you."

Mary was standing next to him in the kitchen, listening to the conversation intently.

Oh my God, please, hurry up. I need to see the doctor.

As he waited for the receptionist to respond, the buzzing inside of him seemed to grow in intensity.

Ka-boom!

He couldn't be sure whether or not it was just his imagination, but in that moment, it felt as intense as it had the night before.

Hurry!

"Okay, so I checked the schedule, and, unfortunately, there aren't any available times open for Dr. Brian to see you today. The earliest time he can see you is nine on Monday morning."

Those words felt like a dagger sliding into his heart.

"No, you don't understand. I **need** to see him. I had a panic attack last night for the first time and I don't know what to do. Please, you have to help me. There must be something available," he begged.

112

There must be something. Please, please. Anything!

"I'm sorry. I've got the schedule pulled up in front of me. There is nothing I can do unless someone else cancels. I'm very sorry."

"So that's it?" he said. His voice was beginning to crack.

Mary grabbed his arm in an effort to calm him.

"I'm very sorry. The earliest we can do is nine a.m., Monday. There is always the walk-in clinic, the E.R., or you could call Telehealth. I am so sorry."

He sighed.

"Okay, that's fine," he said, defeated. He felt like crying then and there.

"Okay, I'll put you in for nine a.m. then. One moment."

There were a few small clicks, and then the receptionist said, "Okay, you're all set for Monday morning."

"Thanks."

He hung up the phone. He felt useless.

What the hell am I supposed to do for three days?

-Nothing.

He shook his head.

"Hey, Joey, it's okay. You'll be okay. Seventy-two hours isn't forever. How about some Calm Tea? You want some?"

He didn't care for anything, but he said, "Yes," anyway.

Mary boiled the kettle.

With nothing else to do, he walked into the living room and slumped down onto the sofa.

What the hell is happening? There was still a ka-boom! in his ear drum. A reminder of his impending doom.

Silvio returned home that evening, and to his surprise, found his son sitting on his couch.

They exchanged a glance, and immediately Silvio could see something was very wrong. His son's eyes were glossy and red, and dark bags bulged and hung beneath.

Mary was in the kitchen, cooking spaghetti for dinner.

"You look like a ghost, son? What's wrong with you?" Silvio said, taking his jacket off and hanging it up.

"I had a panic attack last night, so I came home."

Mary shuffled in from the kitchen, ready to mediate.

"A panic attack? I don't understand. Why? What were you doing? Drugs?"

He breathed out. This is exactly what he wanted to avoid.

Maybe it's just better to tell the truth...

"Just weed, Dad. I've been smoking weed for a long time now. I'm not sure if it was laced with something. It suddenly just stopped working. It gave me a panic attack. I can't explain it. It's like nothing I've ever felt. My body is still messed up. I feel awful."

You didn't mention the cocaine though.

Or all the liquor. Or mushrooms.

"He's got a doctor's appointment, Monday at nine a.m.," Mary said, chiming in.

Silvio looked over at him and shook his head. He then walked over to Mary and kissed her on the cheek. Afterwards, he went downstairs to grab his homemade wine for dinner.

The patriarch was home.

When Silvio returned from the basement, he looked over at him and paused.

"*Figlio,* I don't know what to say."

He turned his tired gaze away from his father.

"I'm sorry, Dad."

⚙

That night, he barely slept. It was the same uneven sleep he had experienced since Thursday. He had taken another melatonin pill and the result had been exactly the same. It only served to make him feel slightly hazy, like the beginning stages of a drug that never progressed. It made his body feel like it was stuck in limbo.

Just like my life, Joey thought.

He glanced at the clock. It was nearly three a.m.

I just want to sleep. Why can't I sleep?

His body's buzzing erupted in response as if to answer his question.

Ka-boom!

He wondered if the buzzing would ever stop. He couldn't sleep or eat. Even during dinner, he was quiet and unresponsive. He barely had four bites of his mother's cooking. Normally, he might have had two plates.

Not once did he feel called to drink or smoke or do drugs of any kind. The thought didn't even cross his mind. He just wanted to get to Monday morning.

I can't wait to get to the doctor. They'll be able to help. I know they will. I know they will…

He fell asleep half an hour later.

His dreams that night were all of being cured.

The weekend was a time for families to spend time together or for kids to stay up late or college students go out to some bar or club. Have fun, unwind. That was now in his past. This time though, his Saturday was spent walking around the block. Over and over again. He didn't particularly want to, but he didn't know what else to do for his pain and turmoil. It hurt more to sit still, so he just kept moving.

Mary had given him a mug of tea to carry with him as he walked.

The neighborhood was big, and each block was about three kilometers long. He kept going in one large loop, his legs seeming to be on autopilot, with him as a reluctant and spaced-out passenger.

Every so often, his pocket would vibrate, and he would take his phone out to see a text or missed call.

There were a few from Niels. He knew he must have been worried about how he was going to pay rent from now on. He knew the Dutch were tolerant types, but this was different.

Hey dude, are you feeling better? We need to talk. I need to know if you're coming back. Are you still at your parents'?

There was another from Anthony.

Hey man, let me know if you need anything.

Similar texts from Marco and John came in as well.

Hey Joey, you can stay with me if you want. I have room.

And,

Hey dude, don't be a stranger. Call me. I can help.

The texts from his friends went on like that, and he was touched they cared, but he could hardly bring himself to reply. When he did, his texts were short, and if he did answer a call, it was over within a couple of minutes. He knew their intentions were good, and he knew Niels would only likely – and quite fairly - be concerned about his part of the rent, but he wasn't in the right frame of mind yet. He only wanted to see the doctor. Everything else was secondary.

He stopped by the house a few times to refill his mug of tea, but other than that he consumed nothing for nearly six hours, from around eight a.m. to two p.m. It was still April, and the winter chills had not yet left the Brampton air. He wore a heavy jacket to stay warm. The buzzing was still unremitting within him, and his mind continued to ask questions, to confront him.

What the hell am I doing with my life? Where do I go from here? Is God punishing me?

It was around two-thirty that his calf seized up. The painful cramp set in halfway around the block. He nearly dropped his mug when it hit him.

Shit!

He paused on the sidewalk to rub his leg with his free hand.

Now the one thing that that was alleviating his pain was also causing more of it.

Remind you of anything, Joey?

He turned around and limped back to the house.

Shut up. Just shut up. JUST PLEASE SHUT UP.

"Thank you for calling Diesel, my name is Jasmine, how can I help you?"

"Hi there, my name is Joey Tomaselli. I used to work there. Do you think I could speak to Jason, please?"

He had called the company he had got fired from the month before to try to ease some of his guilt. He couldn't shake the feeling of divine punishment.

"Oh, okay, yes. I remember you. I will transfer you now."

Background music began to play. It was Sam Cooke's *A Change is Gonna Come*.

He listened to the bittersweet melody for a half a minute or so before Jason answered.

"Hello, this is Jason speaking. How can I help you?"

"Hi, this is Joey Tomaselli. I worked for you guys last month. You let me go."

There was a brief pause.

"Ah yes, Joey. What can I do for you?"

You can take away my pain, a voice thought.

"Nothing actually, Jason. I'm just calling to apologize to you. When I worked there, I really didn't know what I was doing. I should have taken things more seriously. It was hard for me to remember all the different types of jeans and their sizes, and I should have applied myself. I feel bad for wasting everyone's time there. You were a good manager, and I'm sorry."

He let the words pour out of him like spilled wine. He barely caught a breath.

"Oh. Well, I appreciate that, Joey. I know it was a lot, but that was the job. I'm sorry it didn't work out, but thanks for the apology and the kind words."

"No problem. Thanks for listening, Jason."

The two said goodbye, and he hung up.

He had already called two friends before to apologize for things he had done to them. There had been little things, like smoking a joint that wasn't his, and some not so little things.

Both had accepted his apology.

Yet his pain remained. Nothing had changed.

Failure.

He couldn't take it. He did the next natural thing that came to him. He cleaned.

He had been walking around in his room while he had made the call to Diesel. His calf pain still hadn't fully gone away, even though a few hours had passed. He had never walked so much in his life. He wasn't sure if it would go away at all. Ever.

He scanned the contents of his room and decided to start with his closet. It was the nearest to him, and he knew it would need the most cleaning.

He opened up its sliding doors, revealing a large mess of old clothes, toys, and boxes filled with papers and old report cards. He went through all of it, determined to clean up his past. He looked over his old report cards and saw the evidence of his failings. There was row after row of 'C's' and 'D's' in every grade.

You see. You didn't have it figured out back then either.

His phone buzzed. He took it out from his pocket and checked it. It was a text from Niels.

Hey man, you have to move back here eventually. I hope you're ok though, pal. We have to talk this out. Call me. Any time. I am your friend.

He put the phone down. He wasn't ready.

I just need to get some help first, Niels. Let me get something first. Then we'll talk.

His cleaning spree continued into the late evening. The sun was beginning to settle behind the trees.

He was cleaning out his car. Both calves were now hurting, and he had begun to get cold sweats. He felt like vomiting several times as he scoured his car for trash and dirt.

I have to get this clean. I have to get this clean. Jesus, is it Monday yet?

After about ten minutes, he got to the back seat of his car, and behind an empty bottle he found a discarded joint. He felt anger rise up from his stomach.

You! You did this to me!

He picked it up, ripped it and threw it as far as he could. He wished he had enough strength to launch it out of the city.

Never again. Never again will I smoke that shit.

He stood outside in the cold, watching the sunset. He could make out the little joint remnants a few yards away in the street, though it was barely visible.

Never again.

He didn't sleep well again that night. The cramps wouldn't go away. The melatonin still wasn't helping. His guilt felt as constant as the buzzing inside, and he still couldn't shake the feeling something bad was happening to him for a good reason.

What did I do? The Girl? Payback? What? Somebody tell me... I am so sorry.

He got no answers.

He fell asleep around four a.m.

He spent Sunday morning walking. His calf pain had gone away marginally, but it soon returned after an hour around the block. He would stop when he could, but as soon as he felt a little worse, he would start up again.

He felt he had no choice. Anything was better than sitting still.

Around noon, he took a long cold shower in an attempt to feel less pain. He figured the frigid water might help him.

He fidgeted in the shower for nearly twenty minutes, half-crying, half-stoic. It was an odd mix. He wasn't sure what he was supposed to be feeling. He only wanted answers. If only he had those, he could allow himself to heal.

It's okay, man. Just one more day. We just have to get through the rest of today. Dad's making barbecue. That'll be good, right?

But he couldn't bring himself to get excited.

✧

He spent the time after the shower, and before the barbecue, watching Silvio in the garden. Mary fussed about in the kitchen, while he sat motionless at the table. He couldn't walk anymore. His calves hurt too much.

Silvio had cooked up a delicious meal for them. There were plates of juicy ribs, corn on the cob, and a big bowl of mashed potatoes. There was also a bowl of salad that Mary had prepared.

His parents ripped into it. He had five or six bites before pushing his plate aside.

"You haven't eaten all weekend," Silvio said.

Mary looked at him. She was frowning.

"I'm just not hungry, Dad."

Silvio put down his food.

"What the hell did you smoke?"

A slight tenseness seemed to spread around the table.

"I told you, Dad. I think it was laced."

Silvio said nothing more about the weed, but he could tell he wasn't convinced.

"Tomorrow at nine, right?" Silvio added.

"Yea," he said.

It couldn't come fast enough.

"Try eating a little bit more, Joey. Please," Mary said. "Do you want some more water?"

He shook his head, but said, "I'll try, Mom."

He looked at his plate. The ribs were barely touched. The salad unbothered. The corn had been bitten in a few places, and two forkfuls of potatoes were gone.

He picked up his fork and pushed it into his salad.

A wave of nausea hit him.

He put the fork back down.

"I can't, Mom. I'm sorry."

He felt like crying.

☼

It was Monday morning. After a two-hour sleep, he woke up at six a.m. He wanted answers.

He was dressed by six-thirty and awaited the appointment impatiently.

By the time Mary woke up, it had felt like a whole day had gone by.

"Do you want some breakfast?" Mary asked him around eight.

He shook his head.

He wasn't hungry. He had barely slept all weekend. His body was in pain, and the buzzing had never stopped.

I just want help, Mom. You know that.

Mary relented and made something small for herself. Thirty minutes later, the two were in the car and headed to the doctor's office.

The appointment was in Brampton, only a ten-minute drive away.

When they pulled into the parking lot at 8:51, he was the first out of the car.

Let's get this over with.

Mary got out of the vehicle, locking it behind her.

"Are you ready, Joey?" she asked.

He nodded.

I'm ready.

Ready for what, Joey?

An answer.

The two began to walk towards the door.

Chapter 9

I'm waiting for my man
26 dollars in my hand
Up to Lexington 125
Feel sick and dirty
More dead than alive
I'm waiting for my man.
—The Velvet Underground

Monday, April 20th

Mary and he walked into the doctor's office side by side. He was anxious. His forehead was beginning to sweat. He wiped at it nervously.

As they entered the small waiting room, a brunette receptionist that he guessed must have been the woman he spoke to over the phone, greeted them warmly.

"Good morning, how can I help you?"

He walked right up to the desk, and said, "Hi there, I'm here to see Dr. Brian. I have a nine o'clock appointment."

"Okay, what's the name?"

"Joey Tomaselli."

The buzzing inside of him was beginning to worsen.

Ka-BOOM!

As the receptionist typed his name in to the computer, he felt a strange pain begin to circulate throughout his body. He felt as if he had been hit by a truck.

"Okay, Mr.Tomaselli, why don't you take a seat and Dr. Brian will be out shortly."

"Ok, thank you," he replied.

He turned around and took a seat in one the lobby's chairs. Mary sat down next to him and placed a gentle hand on his shoulder.

"It will be okay," she said in a quiet tone.

He nodded, though he wasn't sure he believed her. He did want to though, but the pain was now making it hard for him to even sit down comfortably.

He looked around the waiting area. They were the only two sitting there.

Dr. Brian suddenly opened up the door that separated the offices from the lobby. He hadn't seen him in a while, but he still remembered the familiar look of the man. He greeted them warmly.

"Hi, Joey, Mary. How are you? Come on in," he said.

Mother and son stood up and exchanged pleasantries with him. However, once they were in the office, and the doctor asked him to explain what was wrong, a floodgate seemed to be opened, and everything inside his mind that had been noodling and dissecting over the past few days, burst forth from his mouth like projectile vomit.

"Last week, I smoked a joint, but the weed actually made me feel worse- actually, weed hasn't been making me feel good for months now – it always did- and around midnight, actually at 11:56, I had this panic attack…

"I've never felt anything like it. I felt dizzy, my heart was racing, and I felt this strange buzzing in my body- I still feel it even now, right now…

"-and it's like this adrenaline, but not in a good way- it's more like a constant anxiety, and I can barely sleep, I'm not hungry, and

I'm sweating a lot- too much- and my body feels as if it was hit by a truck, so I don't know what's going on- I'm hoping you can tell me...

"I just need some help, anything will do. I need something."

"Uh-uh," the doctor said calmly. He adjusted his glasses.

"Well, I think the best course of action is to take twelve days to see if anything changes, and then if nothing does, I can give you Lorazepam."

He was hoping to get something now. He was seeing things through a prism of his pain and frustration.

"My whole body is in pain. I can't wait twelve days."

"Yes. However, waiting twelve days is recommended for this type of thing. It may be nothing."

"But I'm in pain. I can't sleep. I don't feel good at all. I need something today," he said, insisting.

"OK, I'm going to set you up with a psychiatrist. Why don't you go and see what he says? He can give you a prescription if he feels it's necessary. Is that fair? I will even try to get you in today."

Mary placed a hand on his knee.

"Will the psychiatrist be able to help?" Mary asked, using the pause to interject.

"Yes, he should be able to," Dr. Brian said.

"Okay, I think that would be good. Joey, do you agree?" Mary asked.

"Sure, go ahead."

They waited as the doctor tapped away on his keyboard and set up an appointment the following day, at one p.m.

"Okay, it's all set up for tomorrow. It is the earliest possible," Dr. Brian said.

Mary and he stood up.

"Thanks, doctor."

Tuesday, April 21st

He sat inside another waiting room. The only difference this time was that there were a few sad faces, scattered around the room with him. He also had brought four pages of notes along, painstakingly prepared the night before, in lieu of sleeping.

He had prepared everything he needed to say.

He kept muttering to himself, going over his lines. Mary sat next to him, watching him carefully from the corner of her eye. She was worried about her only son. She had to drive him everywhere these days. He was too on edge, and in too much pain.

"Mr. Tomaselli?"

He looked up at the slim doctor, standing in the opened doorway who had called his name. He had white hair and a patchy beard.

"That's me," he said, standing up.

"Come on back. Just you, please," the doctor said. "He's in good hands," he smiled at Mary.

Joey looked down at his mom, as he got up.

"Wish me luck," he said.

Mary flashed a reassuring smile.

He followed the doctor through the narrow hallway until they reached the man's office, a sparsely decorated room of dark browns and greys.

"Take a seat. Joey, right?" the psychiatrist said, taking a seat in a comfortable-looking leather chair.

"Yep."

He took a seat opposite the man.

"So, why don't you tell me what's going on?"

"Yea, no problem."

Okay, I'm going to read over these notes. I'm ready for this. Just go over what you practiced, he thought.

He took a deep breath. He flipped to the first page of his notes and began reading.

"Last year I broke up with my long-term girlfriend of seven years. That was hard for me to do because I loved her."

There was a slight pause as tears begin to run down his face. After a deep breath, he continued.

"But she wanted to get married, and I didn't feel I was ready yet. I just felt I wasn't free enough. Since then, I've done a lot of drugs, such as cocaine, marijuana, and sometimes mushrooms. I've been drinking, partying, and smoking.

You're doing great, Joey, keep at it, he thought.

"Last Thursday, I had a massive panic attack after smoking a joint, and it made me feel awful. It was like-"

Joey read out his notes. He got to the end.

The doctor waited for him to finish, then nodded his head, and in one fluid motion produced a prescription pad from one of his drawers.

"I believe you're clinically depressed. I can glean that much. When you've been doing things as long as I have, you begin to recognize it right away."

He began to scribble something across the pad, and then ripped it out and shoved it towards Joey.

"Here's a prescription for Prozac. It will help with the depression, and any anxiety you have."

"I don't get it. I don't think I'm depressed. It was a panic attack," he said.

"I recognize the signs. The drugs, the partying, the break-up, and then the catalyst with the panic attack. It's clinical depression," he said, emphasizing the last sentence.

He placed the slip of paper on the edge of the desk for him to take.

"Are you *sure*?" he asked.

"Very," came the reply.

"Ok, I guess."

He grabbed the prescription and stuffed it into his pocket.

"Give that to your primary care doctor, or a pharmacist, and he or she will fill your medication."

"So that's it?" he said.

"That's it. Thank you for coming in, and I hope this really helps. Come back and see me any time. I am here to help you."

If someone had pointed out to him the irony of having to wait for prescription drugs when he had been doing illegal ones all his life, it would have missed him completely. He was also completely ignorant to the fact he could, at any point, go to any Shoppers' Drugmart or any Rexall to collect his prescription, but his family doctor had said twelve days, and so he intended to wait. It was a self-induced prison, and he had the keys to release himself. But *NOW*, he was following the rules.

✧

He was sitting on the living room couch watching the sports channel, a hot cup of tea in his hand. He had been planted there for over two hours. Three days had passed since the last appointment, and it had been nothing short of agony. He had tried his best to make good use of the time, but when there is nothing to do but wait, time seems to stretch out endlessly like the ocean. He had been going for walks religiously, and with great fervor. This could only soak up so much excess energy, and when he got home, all he wanted to do was sit and stare at the TV. He barely ate, and his sleep schedule was riddled with cold sweats and bad dreams. He was beginning to think that a full eight hours of rest was impossible.

"What are you doing, Joey?" Silvio said, coming up from the basement with a bottle of wine. It was almost dinnertime, though he didn't feel hungry.

"Just watching TV, Dad."

He couldn't bring himself to face his father.

"It's been hours."

Silvio stated the fact with some regret in his voice. Joey could hear it, but he didn't know what to say. His body was still in pain.

I'm sorry, Dad. I just want to sit here, he thought.

"I know," he said. "I did walk a lot earlier, I promise."

The atmosphere of the house had now become tense. Silvio cared, he knew that, but it wasn't easy for the tough, older Italian man to watch his son in mental anguish. He was the strong, silent type.

Sighing, Silvio walked away.

On the TV, the Maple Leafs had just lost the deciding game to see if they would make it into the playoffs.

His phone began to buzz in his pocket. He took it out and looked at the tiny screen.

'Incoming call: Niels.'
He let the phone continue to buzz in his hand. The pain ratcheted up.

The next morning, before noon, some family friends stopped by the house. News had spread that he was back at home, and while the details of his return hadn't been revealed in their entirety, Mary had been forced to tell people something, and it wasn't good. People knew he had suffered some kind of defeat, though they weren't sure of exactly what. Mary wasn't one to gossip, but she also wasn't one to lie. Especially to family.

The doorbell rang, and as soon as he heard it, he bounded towards his room.

He didn't have the courage to face anyone at the moment. Instead, he listened from behind the door.

"Where's Joey?"

"Oh, I think he's sleeping," Mary said in a cheerful voice.

Please don't come and get me, please don't come and get me.

He was thankful that he was left alone.

It was like that almost every day. Someone would come and visit, and he would hide away.

The second night home, his grandmother had come over, and he was happy to at least say hello. He had to avert his eyes the entire time, their glazy red downcast towards the ground. The last thing he remembered seeing on her face was a look of sadness. It was the last thing he wanted to see from his *nonna.*

We are about to meet this amazing lady. Bookmark this.

What am I going to do? he thought.

What can I do? Do I really just have to wait? Do nothing?

He sighed. He grabbed his phone and went through the messages. The rumors had already started.

Hey man, I heard you weren't doing too good. What happened?

Hey Joey, You had a panic attack? Is that true?

Dude, what's happening? Someone said you lost your shit? WTF?

The texts were seemingly endless. He replied to barely any of them. It was too much work to defend himself to everyone. He would hunker down.

What do these people want from me? I'm just trying to survive.

He scrolled down to a recent text from Niels.

Joey, the end of the month is here soon, man. When are you coming back? What am I going to do about rent? I HOPE YOU ARE OK, MAN.

I don't know, Niels. I don't fricking know.

On the fifth day, his impatience reached its peak. It was around dusk when it happened.

Enough is enough. I should just go back to Niels. What am I doing waiting around here? I'm almost twenty-nine. This is bullshit!

He got up from his spot on the couch and headed into the kitchen.

"Mom, I'm going back to Niels. I can't stay here anymore."

Mary looked up from behind the counter. She was cutting vegetables for dinner.

"Are you sure?" she said. He could tell she didn't think it was a good idea.

"I'm sure. I'm ready. I feel better now."

As if to prove that he didn't, his own body began to ache, sending a spike of pain up his spine. He winced.

"Okay, Joey. Do you need help?" Mary asked.

He shook his head.

"I got this. Thanks, Mom."

He headed out of the kitchen and down the hall to his room.

Yes, this is the Joey I know. Getting shit done! he thought.

He began to pack without delay. He shoved his clothes into his suitcase as fast as he could.

Anything miscellaneous was thrust into one of the luggage's many pockets.

Okay, man. We got this. Everything is going to be just fine.

Will it, though?

Yes, yes, it will be. Yes, it will be.

He headed out of his room and made for the front door.

"I'm just going to put this stuff in my car, I'll be right back to say goodbye," he said, as he opened the front door. The evening air was refreshing. The sun was nearly settled over the tree line.

Okay, I feel good.

He walked over to his car, feeling the anxiety and chronic pain leave him for the briefest of moments. He smiled. He unlocked his car and opened up the driver's side door. Then, like the flick of a light switch, he knew he was going nowhere.

What the hell am I doing? I can't even drive. My mom has to drive me everywhere. My whole body hurts. I can't go back to that apartment. I feel bad that Niels needs the money, but I just can't do it.

He let his suitcase fall to the ground at his feet. A gentle breeze seemed to caress his face as he stood there, hopelessness creeping up from his gut.

That's right. Get back in the house where you feel safe. You aren't going anywhere.

He closed the door to his car. He had to fight back tears.

Turn around.

He turned around.

Now, go back in there and take a seat. The game is starting.

Which game? he asked himself. Does it matter?

He did as he was told.

His moment of triumph was just that- a moment.

Friday, May 1st

On day eleven, he thought he had clearly lost weight. He weighed himself as if to calibrate his horror. The near constant walking, and the lack of appetite had left him ten pounds lighter.

Mary had done her best to keep him fed, calm, and feeling loved, but he was a spiritual island away from everyone. Silvio could only watch from afar. He was, in his own way, just as confused as his boy.

The rumors that had spread about him possibly having lost his mind hurt. He had grown up with these people, and suddenly they were gossiping about him, treating him like some TMZ news story.

The enforced patience of having to wait for his meds had taken its toll. For whatever reason, it seemed, he was always waiting to get drugs. His sights were now set on day twelve.

Tomorrow, everything will be okay.

But will it? Hang on. Tomorrow is Saturday. I bet they're closed tomorrow. After that is Sunday.

The realization hit him like a sucker punch to the gut.

He called and checked. The voicemail confirmed the opening hours.

He would actually have to wait fourteen days. He had forgotten that he had a prescription he could use any time, such was his confusion.

No, no, this can't be happening. I have to wait another two days?

The anxiety started back up. He shifted in his bed, looking at the clock. It was almost one a.m.

Please, no more waiting, I can't do it.

I can't do it anymore.

He didn't fall asleep until three-thirty in the morning.

Monday, May 4th

Mary again waited outside in the car. It felt like the right thing to do; to be close and supportive, while encouraging some independence.

He walked into Dr. Brian's office on Monday morning with dark circles under his eyes. His body ached all over, and he was having trouble stifling any yawns.

He figured he had needed the approval of his family doctor before getting the medication he needed. He walked up to the front desk for the second time in two weeks and told the receptionist he was here.

"Just have a seat for now, Mr.Tomaselli. He'll be out shortly," the woman replied.

He nodded and took a seat. He was the only one in the lobby. He had made sure to come first thing in the morning.

Okay, Joey. Let's do this.

A few minutes went by before Dr. Brian opened the door. He took one look at him, and clearly saw his pain.

"Come on back, Joey," the man said.

The two walked down the hallway together, and when they were finally alone, Joey spoke first, taking the prescription from his pocket and handing it over.

"I waited the twelve days, fourteen in fact, just like you said. Am I good now?"

Dr. Brian rubbed his beard, taking a look over the little prescription paper.

"Your symptoms are still the same?"

"Yes. Even worse, actually."

"Okay, well, if the psychiatrist prescribed this Prozac, then I trust his judgment. However, I want you to start taking Lorazepam first and see how it goes before we try Prozac. It's a little bit milder. I'll fax this over to your pharmacy."

"Okay, thank you," he replied, standing up.

The two shook hands.

Later that morning...

He stood in line at the pharmacy counter in Shoppers Drug Mart

There was a big lady with a runny nose behind him, blowing it every few seconds.

In front of him was a tall man with a cast over his forearm, impatiently tapping his foot, waiting for the pharmacist to give him what he needed.

He could relate.

I've waited so long for this. Just a little while longer. Then, I'll be free of

this pain and anxiety. This constant buzzing will finally stop. I'll be able to sleep again. Jesus, I hope I'll be able to eat. I miss my mom's cooking.

He started to reminisce about what it was like before the panic attack.

I was so much freer then. I was doing whatever I wanted, he thought. But where did it get you?

"Next," A voice said, tearing him away from his unanswered thought.

He moved up in line and handed his I.D to the girl.

"I'm here to pick up for Joey Tomaselli."

The girl typed his name into the computer keyboard.

"Ah yes, for Lorazepam, correct?"

"Yes."

"Okay, we have your prescription ready. One moment, please."

He watched her walk to the back and check a section along a long shelf. After a few moments, she grabbed a little white bag, and headed back to the front.

Oh my God, yes, this is it. This is finally it.

His bowels were on edge, as if he were buying an eight-ball of blow.

"Okay, here you go. Are you aware of the side effects, and how to take it?"

"Yes," he said. He didn't care if it gave him horns on his head. He just wanted the anxiety and the pain to go away.

"Okay, here you go. Have a great rest of your day."

"You too, thanks," he replied.

He left and began to open the bag as he walked down the aisle.

Here we go. I had to wait fourteen days for this shit. Seventeen from the actual time of the attack.

He took out the orange pill bottle and examined it in his hand. It was half-filled with little white tablets. He walked to the front of the store, grabbed a bottle of water from the little fridge by the register, and joined the line. Finally, the man behind the counter rang up his purchase, and he paid in cash.

As soon as he left the store, he unscrewed the lid to the pill bottle and placed one in his hand. It was tiny, but Joey sensed and anticipated its delicious potency.

He placed it inside his mouth, and then took the cap off the water bottle, and took a big gulp, washing the tablet down his throat.

The effect was almost immediate. The anxiety stopped. The buzzing calmed. The pain would soon subside slightly. Soon, his hunger would also return. His eyes widened. He even cracked a smile. For the first time in over two weeks, he felt the pull of peace.

It was like that first joint all those years ago.

FREEDOM!

Sweet freedom.

PART FOUR
LEGAL DRUGS

Chapter 10

Antidepressants have been noted to **cause hallucinations**, often with drug overdose, but also in rare instances as a side effect at therapeutic dose. Bupropion, tricyclics, and selective serotonin reuptake inhibitors (**SSRIs**) have most often been cited as the causative agents. Auditory and Complex Visual **Hallucinations** (CVH) are rare adverse effects with ingestion of SSRIs, including **fluoxetine**, sertraline, fluvoxamine, paroxetine, and citalopram that are most often presented as case reports in the literature.

(British Medical Journal, October 1999)

✿

here's no ka-boom! There. Is. No. Ka-boom! There is no fricking ka-boom!

    Joey felt the ecstatic rush, the euphoria, the unadulterated rapture of feeling kind of normal. It was the same ultimate relief one feels when the worst hangover in the world has gone, and one is simply able to walk to the fridge or flip the channel without a warning from God that one's head might implode. Ah, the simple things.

These are the everyday pleasures we take for granted and seem a million miles away when we feel a lump in an armpit or stumble across an errant and uneven mole on the skin. Just to be normal is, in these circumstances, a worthy excuse to prompt a solar plexus scream to let the world know that we are all right. If only we could maintain this level of joy – just from feeling ok - forever. Three days after an all-clear biopsy, most of us are growling at bad drivers and frowning at cyclists on the pavement once again. Is this the key to life?

I will be grateful forever. I promise.

Mary was driving him home, and she glanced over at him from time to time. She made it seem as though she was checking for traffic, so as not to exert undue pressure. He knew what she was doing, and it made him happy. It was easier to be happy now that he didn't have to hear the percussion of his own heartbeat, thumping like a kick drum in his inner ear. Most things seemed easier to achieve now that that abysmal noise had left his head. Each thump had seemed like a reminder of his own mistakes and weaknesses, each rush of blood through his system hacking at his now-flimsy spirit. It had been weeks now, and there was no way of calibrating how much his central nervous system had been battered like a flimsy old rowboat in a relentlessly bruising Atlantic hurricane.

But spring was now here, matching the trajectory of Joey's mood step-for-cautious-step. The jaunty and mild morning, with her soft azure backdrop and sheepskin clouds, was unassuming. She announced herself, mildly confident but nowhere near a swagger. Just happy to be here, just glad to feel normal too, her vicious and Arctic winter hangover a thing of the very recent past.

Maybe spring was here before? Maybe I did not notice? Or is life just lovely enough for this to be a coincidence?

Mary saw him smile, as he leant to look out of the passenger side window at budding trees and he lowered his window to stick his head out like an ecstatic hound to feel the enveloping breeze. She said nothing. All in good time. Her own optimism – similarly battered by that robust storm – was stirred. She believed in him, and this latest development felt right, but she was a wise and sage enough barometer to know that an improvement does not suggest a cure. One thing at a time, she thought. One step at a time. A mother knows.

And so, a comfortable silence was maintained until Mary pulled into the drive and switched off the engine. She turned, saw a quarter smile on her son's lips, and touched his knee to indicate her support and hope. They opened their own doors and made for the sanctuary of the family home.

Once inside, she asked him if he'd like a cup of tea, the one that helped him to relax.

"No, thanks, Mom. I feel fine without one. I really feel different. The noises in my head have gone. I knew I needed something. He *could* have done this two and a half weeks ago."

"Well, we have it now."

He loved that Mary used the word, *we*.

This is her fight too, he thought. I love her so much. Thanks, Mom. The words of a song drifted through his head. 'Mother Mary comes to me.'

I have something to do, he thought.

And he walked to the living room, where he sat down with a steady determination. And he thought about whom to call first. He recalled how good it had felt when he'd contacted his old boss to apologise.

Time to start to say sorry, Joey. Who is going to be first?

He reckoned he had maybe a dozen calls to make as a fair starter.

Then I am going to do something to really make that amazing lady in the kitchen happy.

I'm going to get a damned job.

Twelve apologies and a new job. Lay THAT one on Silvio at dinnertime as I shovel down three plates of pasta.

Hang on first. Just one thing before I do all of that. Let me have another one of those little pills. It is almost lunchtime.

So, he went into his jean pockets, pulled out his latest salvation, his new best friend – just as weed had once been – and nudged out one into his palm before sweeping it onto his tongue and down it went without water.

Now, where was I?

Yes, redemption. But redemption – and its pal, respect - must be earned. He thought of how Silvio and Mary had always told him that everyone deserves a second chance. Third and fourth chances are harder to wriggle and wrest out of people. But anything short of murder or premeditated viciousness is likely to find a welcoming ear, especially if it is freely offered and without compulsion. This made Joey happy, and he sensed already that it would feel good to apologise. But he reminded himself he was not doing this for himself. That would simply pull the rug out from under his intentions. This was for *them*. This was for the people he had wronged, upset or lied to.

Yes. This is not about me.

He picked up his phone, scrolled to contacts and started at the letter A.

✿

Chemical formula $C_{15}H_{10}Cl_2N_2O_2$ - Lorazepam, sold under the brand name Ativan among others, is a benzodiazepine medication.[3] It is used to treat anxiety disorders, trouble sleeping, active seizures, including status epilepticus, alcohol withdrawal and chemotherapy-induced nausea and vomiting. It is also used during surgery to interfere with memory formation and to sedate those who are being mechanically ventilated. While it can be used for severe agitation, midazolam is usually preferred.[3] It is also used, along with other treatments, for acute coronary syndrome due to cocaine use.[3] It can be given by mouth or as an injection into a muscle or vein.[3] When given by injection onset of effects is between one and thirty minutes and effects last for up to a day.

(Wikipedia)

He made twelve calls by the time Silvio came home, which was twenty minutes after his third Lorazepam that day. Nine calls were answered – three made wise cracks about Tony Soprano and his meds -, and he left three voicemails. Each had ended cordially. There was also a strong chance of a job with a friend of Silvio's, an Italian lady who lived on their street and who had a construction business. Her name was Mrs. Rossi.

These drugs are very good. Boy, am I looking forward to a fine night's sleep? Ten hours uninterrupted. I think I deserve that. One of those cups of calm tea Mom makes. Tazo. The one with the snuggly teddy bear on the box. Sleep like a baby. Yes.

The third pill was working like a charm.

The sense of self-satisfaction and hope came in waves, as he wondered how much was reality and how much was the impact and efficacy of the drug? He shrugged and realised it didn't really matter. The banging in his head had gone, the voices had gone and even the pain in his calf had subsided. For the first time since he could remember, there was a reason to be hopeful. Even the sore feeling he had around Niels and the apartment seemed as if it was on the point of a resolution.

So what? I will lose my deposit, but he has found a new roommate, and it seems like he – the kind friend - might understand how messed up I was. How messed up I may still be. Don't get carried away, Joey. Don't get carried away!

Guess what. Joey got carried away. And it was alcohol that did it. The wolf in sheep's clothing. Or as Mary liked to call it, '*The wolf in wolf's clothing.*'

One week after the prescription was filled, Joey took his first drink – vodka and soda - since it had all gone down. Perhaps the drugs had been too good and had convinced him he was on a really steady footing. Perhaps the joy in feeling normal again had been a reason to go out and celebrate as if one were lifting the Ontario Cup in a sweaty and partially bloodied Woodbridge Strikers jersey. And then things started to get really cloudy, for at the end of that seemingly pivotal month, he had Prozac to add to his Lorazepam.

The cards were dealt. The future was set. Now just add time. Inevitable, mean and unforgiving. Time.

❖

Fluoxetine, sold under the brand names **Prozac** and **Sarafem** among others, is an antidepressant of the selective serotonin reuptake inhibitor (SSRI) class.[2] It is used for the treatment of major depressive disorder, obsessive-compulsive disorder (OCD), bulimia, nervosa, panic disorder, and premenstrual dysphoric disorder. [2] It may decrease the risk of suicide in those over the age of sixty-five. Fluoxetine is taken by mouth.

Common side effects include indigestion, trouble sleeping, sexual dysfunction, loss of appetite, dry mouth, rash, and abnormal dreams.[2] Serious side effects include serotonin syndrome, mania, seizures, an increased risk of suicidal behaviour in people under twenty-five years old, and an increased risk of bleeding.[2] If stopped suddenly, a withdrawal syndrome may occur with anxiety, dizziness and changes in sensation.[2] It is unclear if it is safe in pregnancy.[6] Its mechanism of action is not entirely clear but believed to be related to increasing serotonin activity in the brain.[2]

(Wikipedia)

Prozac generally takes two to three weeks to begin to be effective. Well, the day he was given the next large batch of pills by the pharmacist, Joey started that new landscaping job.

An eight-hour work out. It will be good for me. Get a sweat on. Physical exercise in the late spring with pals. Perfect, he thought. Like a training session with the Strikers. Remember how good that felt afterwards?

Well, it all seemed to make sense, but the damage was already done. The beast of alcohol in the mix had upset the balance, a ticking time bomb. The silent and seemingly harmless stuff available on most street corners in liquor stores, cafes, bars and restaurants. The most vicious and malevolent of the toxins available to us; booze. Lorazepam on her own might have been fine, but liquor meant Prozac was needed too, and that is when Joey began to feel truly afraid, as the juggler is thrown a third flaming torch to lob up and catch and repeat. *Ad infinitum.* Well at least until something goes wrong.

June 4th, 2009

It was the day he was shifting mounds of earth in the early prep for a big job in a country house in Aurora.

Mrs. Rossi had built a successful construction company and had now gladly offered Joey the chance to get outside, do some graft, earn some cash and perhaps, just perhaps, feel good about himself. It was his third week there, and maybe the third job he had done with her. This new job was a three-week gig, a lot of work. There was forestry, lawns, flower beds on the fringes of a large-ish ravine. The sun was strong, the sky cloudless. Barely a breath of air was to be felt. One of the building crew, Johnno was working with him that morning, but had momentarily gone inside to use the bathroom. Joey was walking down the long driveway when it happened. He felt a strange and gentle fluttering in his head, as if he had stood up too quickly. It felt perhaps like a rush of a chemical, as if autumn leaves were blowing around inside his skull or baby mice scuttling across taut greaseproof paper.

Jesus!

Startled, he leapt backwards, dropping his shovel, staggering, and almost falling into a hole.

What's a fricking hyena doing here?

TWO of them. Jesus Christ. JESUS!

He saw them run to his either flank. He covered his face. Would

143

they come for him? They looked hungry. They looked angry. If they came from either side of him in a coordinated attack, he wouldn't stand a chance. He needed that shovel. He removed his hand from his face, and they were not there anymore. The larger, toothier hyena, the seemingly hungrier one, had scuttled away, but he felt as if they were preparing to attack him should he fall. They like to scavenge on a corpse. Even better if the blood inside is still warm. The voices – yes, now a dialogue - started inside his head.

'What? Careful. Have they gone? Did you see them run off?'

'What are you talking about, Joey?'

'The hyenas. They were there. Not ten feet from where you're standing.'

'You're losing it, man.'

'I don't know which I'd prefer. For them to be real or imaginary. Neither is good.'

He shook his head, slapped his face, and sat down on a rock by the driveway to gather himself.

He took several deep gulps of air and reached into his pocket for a pill. He took a Lorazepam. He then stretched his torso out and tried to encourage the flow of blood around his system. He began to give himself a pep talk. He took over one of the voices in his head.

'Breathe. It's ok. It's ok. Breathe. Think good thoughts. This is good for you.'

Johnno called him from the lobby of the house.

'Hey, man! Are you ok? Can you give me a hand with this cabinet in here, Joey?'

'Yeah, sure. Of course,' Joey said. 'I am coming.'

Perhaps he should have considered this response, but he did not want to let his team down. He walked inside the vast front entrance and breathed in the scent of polished tiles floors. The echo inside was the echo of wealth. He kicked off his boots and followed Johnno to a mezzanine level. Down a lengthy corridor he went, ten yards behind his work pal, and ushered along by the lady owner, who had been kind to them for the four days they had been there.

'This cabinet, I need it to be taken to the front driveway, please, boys.'

'Of course,' Johnno and Joey said in unison.

'Please be careful with it though.'

The guys took an end each and found the centre of gravity of the piece, hoisted it to hip height and began to inch it down the dark hallway back to where they had come.

It was heavy, but manageable. Joey should have breathed in more air, found a sturdier footing after his hallucination – yes, it *must* have been an hallucination -, and, more than anything, he needed the oxygen. He started to feel wobbly again.

Oh Jesus. I need to sit down. I think I can hear that damned drumbeat again. Oh no, say it's not coming back. Oh Jesus. It's coming back.

'Stop,' he shouted through tight lips. 'I need to...'

He wanted to speak of the pain in his chest.

I'm having a fricking heart attack. I cannot breathe. It's my chest.

He saw stars for a split second, and then it started again.

'Ka-boom! Ka-boooooom!' Ka-booooooom!'

'KAAA-BOOOOOM!'

'Oh god no. Please. No. I can't breathe. The ground. I can't breathe.'

The tilted cabinet remained at forty-five degrees, as Joey slumped slowly to the tiles. He did not fall, but there he now sat in a sad heap, holding his chest, his eyes narrowed and fearful.

'Jesus, Joey, man. Are you ok?' Johnno said.

'Oh my. Should I call an ambulance?' the lady asked.

He could not speak for now, but his hand gesture seemed to suggest to the others that he just needed a minute. He needed more than that, but when he had gulped in enough air to speak, he managed to splutter out, 'Just call Mrs. Rossi, please. I just need to go home.'

Mrs. Rossi soon witnessed the veins bulging in Joey's neck and saw the red capillaries all join hands in the whites of the poor boy's eyes, so she was immediately sympathetic.

'Please just drive me home. I... I... I...'

She drove him home.

✪

The next day was his twenty-ninth birthday party. It was July the 9th, 2009. He felt somewhat guilty that he had left the job but was still able to host an event.

He was welcoming friends onto the patio of the *Muzik* nightclub in downtown Toronto. He had a VIP section cordoned off. He was still feeling somewhat fragile.

Breathe, boy. You've got this. Everyone is here for you tonight. Shoulders back. Chin up. Chest out. Push forward.

There was a surprise visitor. The Girl. It had been perhaps six months since he had called her on the phone out of the blue. His search for comfort had turned on itself quite disastrously. He remembered that she had picked up first time. He wanted comfort and to let her know he was suffering, but each time he tried to coax it out of her, he was met with a straight bat, for The Girl too needed something. She wanted to let him know that her suffering had dwarfed his. And still did. He had known then that the call had been a mistake. But she did want to meet and try to work it out. He wanted comfort, she wanted answers.

Oh shit, I am so sorry. I keep hurting you. You do not deserve this. Why did I do that? That was so selfish.

And there she was now, hovering near on the edge of the dance-floor with her two friends. Hoping against hope. Looking beautiful. Deserving more.

I need a drink. I need a big fricking drink.

'Hey birthday boy, you need a drink?'

'Jesus, yes, please. Triple vodka and soda, please.'

And he went into the hip stitch pocket of his jeans and took out his third Lorazepam of the day.

Despite a proclivity to rely on his new medication, Joey was supremely capable of holding his liquor. That night, he drank too much, and yet remains still remarkably clear-eyed about the evening's events. We all know characters who possess this enviable skill. Joey's friends rarely knew if he was drunk. He held a steady grip on his words, his gait, and his expression. He had even had police officers give him his keys back after a day of partying, unaware that he was beyond gone.

And so, he can recall each of the friends, former friends and girlfriends who turned up. He can remember where each hung out, the records that played, the gifts he received and the sweet kisses on his stubbly cheek from very pretty women. He can recall how The Girl observed each one who leant in for a lingering peck. He can see her now in that little black dress, and he can recall her *Carthusia Fiori di Capri* perfume in his nostrils. It seemed that she knew this might lure him so seductive is the glorious tang. The Italians knew how to make perfume back in the day. She had done her homework. Could she now hypnotize him as she had once pretended to be entranced for that notorious lap dance so, so long ago? It would provide a neat symmetry would-that-it-were so. But Joey did not believe in that kind of magic.

He knew that when she offered to drop him off at *their* place on The Queensway – the place to where they should have returned after their honeymoon – it was not the best idea. Her friend, her very gorgeous friend, drove the black Honda Civic that should, had The Girl had her way, have been parked under that building while they shared their conjugal bed in marital bliss. But it was not to be.

He sat in the back, dazed, full of booze and now only droopy eyed through fatigue and yes, perhaps the culminative effect of the liquor, Lorazepam and the Prozac. But still he recalled the whole chat. Perhaps it was the fact that she could not provoke any kind of passion or excitement or reaction from him that she became so frustrated that the final act in that pivotal evening was to turn from the passenger seat and throw a full bottle of water in his steady and unperturbed face. She desperately wanted and sought a reaction. There was nothing. Joey remained calm and unflustered.

'Goodbye,' he said.

At least anger would have indicated some sliver of emotion, some nerve-end or passion of any kind, but there was naught.

Feeling both shocked and utterly impotent at his impassiveness, was this her final and parting shot?

147

The girls left him at the side of the road.
Arrivederci, handsome. Maybe in the next life, birthday boy...
And *that* was that.

The hangover the next morning was a bastard-behind-the-eyes. Is it strictly a hangover if one does not sleep? At 8 a.m. the next morning, on his twenty-ninth birthday, he again got into his car and drove to the womb of his family home, that shining *castello* on the mythical hillside in the independent state of Silvio and Mary Tomaselli.

The meltdown that started that morning would last for several weeks and plumb new depths. Joey Tomaselli would now set in motion a journey - through a seemingly untold and ceaseless number of medical professionals of varying efficacy, decency and quackery – that would take him to the saddest of destinations; one that no parent should have to confront. But we rush ahead. Let us return to the poor boy's birthday.

His eyes revealed how very messed up he was as he walked once again defeated to the front door.

Here we go again. I am not sure how I can dig my way out of this one. Perhaps better not to dig. Perhaps better to let the soil come on in, fall on my face, and have done with this torture forever. KA-BOOOOOM!

Chapter 11

There he was once again. Walking around the block. The precise same sidewalks from the horror of early spring. The hope that came in waves with the thawing of the tundra was now a distant and punctured dream. The honeymoon that never was. A lonely young man going nowhere. There and back to see how far it was. Hunched. Hollow. An air of desperation in the slack gait that would soon be mirrored in the falling of brown and crispy leaves just as the green clitoral buds of May had heralded in blooming hope. The nights were already drawing in, hope had reached its zenith already. ALL DOWNHILL FROM NOW. Life imitating nature. Nature mimicking the sad excuse of a kind and once-hopeful boy's life. If May had felt like a regression in his return to the womb of the familial home, then this felt like a capitulation.

All of that for nothing. Two steps forward, three back.

And still the lady in the kitchen stood robustly behind him, determined, instinctive, instinctual. The Nat Geo docco. It is what she does, unthinking. It is impossible to gauge the importance of this in his mind. We just sense that without it, *without her,* he would be gone. She is the last line of defence. The lioness who paces the cage with her young. The cage is there to protect **us.** Love knows no bounds.

Ka-boom! Ka-boooom! Ka-booooooom!

The weekend was a carbon copy of that mid–April anguish. No sleep, no food, long walks, projecting to nine a.m. on Monday morning when the pleading call to the doctor's office would be made. He was all alone all day on Sunday as the family went to a confirmation. He was grateful for this space and this small mercy. He continued with the Lorazepam. They had worked for a while. The Prozac however had only brought troubling issues and pain. He ditched these in the trash. A ceremonial and aggressive pitch into the garbage. Still the anguish would not abate.

Help me! M'aidez! M'aidez! HELP ME! MAN DOWN!

Monday 9:01 EST

Joey got through to the receptionist first time. Mary sat by him at the kitchen table. The early sun warmed the house from the east. One more small mercy came in the form of a gap in Dr. Brian's schedule that afternoon at 2.45.

The day continued as had the weekend. The hangover may have diminished, but the headache persisted, as did the blurred vision, the dazed feeling and the utter hollowness of spirit.

Damned torture. Ka-boom! Ka-boom! Ka-boom!

His inner ear drummed out the rhythm of his pain, regret, remorse and unabashed misery. Relentless. The torture shall not cease.

Mary went with him to the doctor. She drove, accompanied him into the reception. He went into the appointment alone. He emerged seventeen minutes later with a slip of paper in his right hand.

> The **escitalopram**, marketed in different countries under the names *Lexapro, Cipralex, Sipralexa* and *Seroplex* is an antioxidant selective serotonin reuptake inhibitor. Escitalopram is used in the treatment of depression and anxiety. Succeeding since 2004 to citalopram, which was the racemic mixture (R form + S form) and had the same

therapeutic action but whose patent had expired, escitalopram (S-citalopram) is chemically its en-antiomer of the pure S form, the only truly active form of the drug. This would also make it possible to dispense with unnecessarily ingesting the R-form and therefore possibly reducing the side effects of a treatment.

(Wikipedia)

He only took one of them, regretted it immediately, and discarded the bottle of anti-depressants. This act concerned Mary to the core. He had not given them a chance. He had merely felt the weight of Groundhog Day.

Basta! BASTA! Enough!

He now sought alternatives to traditional medicine. Even the names given to these threads of help were enough to turn the corners of Silvio's mouth down to the ground in that independent state, that small-ish quadrant of Italy in Brampton, Ontario.

Therapy, hypnotism, life coach.

'Give me a break,' the old man might have said as he left the kitchen, perhaps just starting to slump like his boy. It would not have happened back in the old country.

There were cliques developing among his friends, and things were going to get worse he feared. It was a microcosm of the land of Italy; a collection of tribes and peoples shoved together under one banner. But really fierce and independent mobs, willing to go toe-to-toe at any time and for almost any reason. Joey sensed that the cracks in the social scene were only going to get nastier and meaner. He was a finely adjusted barometer. He knew. He heard whispers coming back of how some friends were bad-mouthing him.

The only other times Joey would leave the Tomaselli homestead in the coming weeks were when he left with Silvio to go work at the car shop. It was a mercy gig. Silvio was throwing him a fatherly bone that would help to fill Joey's days, earn some cash, and possibly bring a father and son closer together. Could something beautiful be salvaged out of this?

The family thought it adorable and mildly amusing (in the kindest possible way) that these two – this unlikeliest of odd couples – were working together. They knew he knew nothing about engines and were warmed to their core to see this union flourish; none more so than Mary.

This symbiosis continued for the rest of July and almost all of August. It was the twenty-ninth when the young man found the name of a therapist in the ads column of the *Toronto Sun* that was delivered to the shop daily. This was professional number two.

This gent was ex-military and in his fifties.

'I can get you off the pills, Joey,' he said on the phone that hot and balmy lunchtime. 'Not only that, but you need only come to me once.'

He liked the sound of that. This man was not interested in a long-term money grab. In which case, what was there to lose?

Well, the respect of his father for one. In a scene that might have hit the cutting-room floor in *The Sopranos*, Silvio again pulled faces and gestured with his palms at the sagacity of a grown man visiting a therapist. What cut even more deeply is that Silvio was paying for it. One hundred and fifty dollars.

'But he says he can fix me in one visit, Dad.'

'Good money after bad. That's what this is.'

The old man peeled off three red fifties from a small wad in his pocket.

'*Bocca al lupo*, son.'

'*Crepi.*'

Cold turkey - The genesis of the phrase is disputed. Perhaps it "comes from the similarities between a drug addict in the throes of withdrawal and a turkey's carcass. Both can be clammy, pale and covered in goosebumps, which might have led someone to point out that a user who suddenly quit looked like a cold turkey."

—Mentalfloss

"**Cold turkey**" refers to the abrupt cessation of a substance dependence and the resulting unpleasant experience, as opposed to gradually easing the process through reduction over time or by using replacement medication.

Sudden withdrawal from drugs such as alcohol, benzodiazepines, and barbiturates can be extremely dangerous, leading to potentially fatal seizures. For long-term alcoholics, going cold turkey can cause life-threatening delirium tremens, rendering this an inappropriate method for breaking an alcohol addiction.

In the case of opioid withdrawal, going "cold turkey" is extremely unpleasant but less dangerous. Life-threatening issues are unlikely unless one has a pre-existing medical condition.

—Wikipedia

Silvio waited at the kitchen table. Mary hustled and bustled around him.

He walked in, and pulled out a chair, slumping into it. Exhausted, but apparently pleased with himself.

They waited for him to speak.

'His advice was pretty clear. I just need to reduce the dose. Daily. Wean myself off the tablets. I am on three pills a day right now and that's too many. Tomorrow I am going to take three halves, two days after that three quarters. Two quarters. One quarter. Get off them in ten days.'

His parents nodded and were impressed by their boy's determination.

'They don't feel like they're working anyway, so how hard can it be?'

Silvio glanced at Mary, who now sat down next to him and held his well-worked hand.

The therapist's theory was always likely to be a kind of sound one, but one must take into account the key variable of the rate of the diminishing dose. Would this prompt cold turkey? In Joey's case, the answer was a most definite **yes.**

There was an immediate and vicious reaction to the reduction, such is the malicious nature of addiction. He was getting no benefit anymore – no upside - but you try to come off them, and they will screw you up. It was the worst of both worlds. No up. Plenty of down.

That's just not fair! Well, it wasn't fair when you dumped that poor girl.

The cold sweats, the hot sweats, the sleepless nights, the shaking. All reminiscent of the more gruesome scenes of *Trainspotting.* Mary's calming *Tazo* tea did not even scratch the surface.

Anguish. Torture. Hell.

The words were emblazoned onto his subconscious. They ran around his head as he tossed and turned and sweated like that squeezed teabag.

At this time and during these night terrors, he sensed like a wounded animal that there was an extra dimension to this horror. He could not put his finger on the issue. Metaphorically or literally. But something nagged at him. There was **something else** going on. This was a visceral and knee-jerk reaction, but he knew his own body, and as much as he sensed there was a problem at hand about which he had no idea, his instinct threw into the mix that just maybe whatever it was he was trying to uncover, might just – in a real Vegas long shot – lead him to the answer to all of this. But he was so unwell this might as well also have been the other thing Vegas can offer – a massive mirage; mean and unforgiving and likely to destroy the soul, leaving him dead in the desert.

✡

He was now alone. Untethered with no safety net, apart from the bottle of Lorazepam, perpetually in his back pocket, like the erstwhile booze hound who keeps an untouched Smirnoff in the top cupboard for a decade or two.

That I will do for the rest of my life.

Well, there was the safety net of his home and his loving parents, but that had limitations for one day he **would** need to leave there.

The pills would be there for a panic attack that might hit at any time like an act of terrorism flashing on the news. Just when you least expect it.

There it is again. I should have known. I need to be on guard. They just need to get through once.

But it was not just the random attacks on his psyche that he needed to defend against. There may be another enemy, plotting and conspiring against him. He feared his old friends had reached the limit of their patience with him. Was he paranoid?

Text messages taken out of context and screenshot and passed around with a different frame each time soon take on the form of Chinese whispers. Or was he imagining this?

I cannot even defend myself. My words are being used against me, and I don't know who has seen them and who hasn't. They are all talking about me.

Ka-booooooom!

✡

And then came the sweats again. And then extremities of hot, cold, hot, cold, soaking his clothes, bedsheets, pillows. There was the

155

nausea that make him puke into a bucket, the sight of the barf bringing on wretches in waves of viciousness, until he was empty, but still the spasms in his gut and oesophagus came, forgetting that there was nothing left to expel. This flicked the hot sweats to cold chills and back again like a breaker board. It was a new intensity of pain, both physical and mental.

How could any drug or drink or cure or painkiller ever be worth this?

He thought of how this is how chemotherapy must feel.

I would be happier as a corpse right now. If I had a blade, I would crawl across broken glass to end it.

Heroin addicts have been known to prevail through this, only to rush to a dealer with notes stolen from a loved one or a TV set from one's grandparent and exchanged for enough to buy a small wrap and to start the whole sorry process again. He wasn't that bad, but he considered the pain of his fellow sufferers. He was, after all, a good son. He did think of others.

Normal life appeared a million miles away. Some altered Universe, some parallel existence where people held down jobs, raised kids, did not need tablets, enjoyed weekends and primetime television dross.

Could I do this again one day? Impossible.

He barfed again and squeezed his wet pillow like a soggy towel.

It was like the Night of the Long Knives as friend after friend messaged him to say they were done with him. He shook. He sweated. He curled up into a ball, a self-protective posture against the bombardment of a truly cruel world.

It's not fair, man. Yes, it is. You brought this on.

Silvio and Mary were away. He managed to get into his car and drive to his sister's house. To Sandra's.

I have been destroyed, Sandra. They've destroyed me.

He had never felt so exposed, so let down. Could he ever show his face socially again?

Even his good friend, Dave - he found out that same night - had made a pass at The Girl. There are times when, "Well you didn't love her" should not be uttered. This was one.

There was one saving grace. At least he did not really feel like taking his own life, he convinced himself. But that was not far in the distance.

✿

In October 2009, another well-meaning girlfriend recommended a hypnotist. People have always got a solution. They are so wise. They know a healer, a shaman, a witch, the best cancer doctor, a wizard. 'Oh! you must see my guy!' They mean well, but… well, you know.

It was the Friday before Thanksgiving weekend.

'Yes, Joey. Come on Tuesday. I promise to fix you.'

'Ok, thanks.'

'You should go out and see your friends too this weekend. It will be good for you,'

There was a pause.

'You don't need to drink. Just be near people you like.'

He focused positively on a possible pending cure. It was not lost on him that it was hypnotism that had brought him the love of The Girl.

✿

And so, he showed up on time and handed over the hundred and fifty bucks.

Is this where dreams are made, and prayers are answered? Give it a chance, Joey. Give him a fair chance.

And so, he walked down the frayed and carpeted staircase with a grim determination to at least keep his mind open to the possibilities.

Just think of how amazing I might feel tomorrow.

This lure was enough to get him there.

Think positively, Joey. Anything is possible. Think of no pain. Think of the ABSOLUTE JOY OF NO PAIN. The ecstatic state of painlessness and silence in my mind. Eye on the prize.

KA-BOOOOOOM!

And it was all going fine until Joey was told to picture himself as a pirate on a sailing ship in the fifteenth century.

'Prepare for battle, Joey.'

Well, **that** was enough. Christopher Columbus may have been Genoa's favourite son and the pride of Italy, but…

Come on, man! Really!

'Please keep the money. This is not for me. I do not mean to be rude. This was a mistake.'

He drove home to hibernate. He was done. For now. He sat with Mary in silence.

There was one more October surprise in store, one that would make the days of earlier that month and that previous summer seem like the glorious past. For he was about to be hit by a millstone that he thought he had summoned to the garbage can of history. He was about to hit by a terror attack, the like of which he had not seen since his childhood. The identity of the perpetrator was a truly malevolent force, and the fact he had not ever prepared for its return just shows how brutal it can be. No shouts of *Allah Akbar!* No burkas. No seventy-two virgins. But a terror attack of horrendous proportions never-the-less. **Obsessive Compulsive Disorder.**

It was October 28th. And another friend who knew best. Yes, Joey was able to have a damned good cry with the life coach, as she felt and kneaded his weak spots in his arms. It was all going so well, until he closed his eyes and let his mischievous imagination go a-wandering. But what in god's sweet name possessed him to think she was about to spray a natural spritz in his mouth?

And there in his mind's eye, a million figurative miles from the reality of it all, a non-existent liquid was sprayed onto his reluctant and fanciful tongue. His OCD came flooding back. The life coach was left confused and worried about him.

Anxiety and depression now had the third element of the mirepoix' OCD. Back to the thirteen-year-old Joey.

JESUS CHRIST!!! KA-BOOOOOOM!

Joey left the session and recoiled to his family to wash his hands perpetually and even develop a phobia of blood.

What was I thinking? I'd give anything to rewind to yesterday.

But it wasn't quite like a return to the thirteen-year-old Joey Tomaselli. His cures were quickly reducing in number. No weed. No Lorazepam. And a whole load of pain in between.

Zero steps forward, four steps back.

I am drowning here. KA-BOOOOM!

Two words, Joey. Two words.

Push forward. Push forward.

That nagging blind-spot in his mind, that foggy and nebulous Vegas mirage perhaps, told him to push forward.

Chapter 12

There he was in Shoppers Drugmart under the harsh strip lights, a contrast to the obsidian night outside. He displayed many of the hallmarks of a demented sort. There was a twitch, eyes darting around avoiding others' concerned frowns and hoping to be out of range of the video cameras, or at least unobserved in some security control room.

'Poor boy,' one old lady with a basket of oatmeal and satsumas muttered to another, laden down with an armload of canned prunes and toilet paper, who shook her creased countenance in concerned agreement.

Fricking red on the floor. Is it blood? It cannot be blood. Can it?

He was trying to avoid the cracks between the faux tiles and also maintain a safe distance from the red lines and arrows that pointed to the pharmacy or to the post office in the back. He now had a phobia of anything red. Especially on floors, in case it was blood, or on the skin, in case it indicated blood near the surface or in a pimple or a scab or a tiny nick. The manifestation of the return of his OCD was the bizarre fear – and a phobia, by definition, is an irrational fear – of blood. Was this a tweaking of his fear of AIDS from the potato chip? Perhaps, it was, but the sharp viciousness of his worry and obvious anguish was enough to lead these two old dears with their evening provisions, as well as any other sane soul who crossed his frenzied path, to worry for him.

A security guard strolled past the end of the aisle and glanced down to notice the troublesome gait. It was not that it was threatening, but something was definitely up. It did not help that he wore no shoes. One might have thought that these would have acted as a barrier against the twin enemies of blood and germs. He had just discarded his third pair of new shoes of the evening. This was his latest stunt, the poor soul. He would walk into the mall, pay for a new pair of shoes, and if the salesperson had a Band Aid or a slightly chewed fingernail or neck pimple, he would take over the credit card terminal, pay, walk out and dump the shoes in the garbage out in the car park. Sometimes he would go back and buy the same pair from the same person if he inadvertently stood near anything red. The eyes darted perpetually and consistently on alert for any shade of rouge, vermillion or scarlet. The back of his jeep was inaccessible, piled up with a dozen and a half shoe boxes. Any bum worth his salt should have shadowed him, Hansel and Gretel style, and transformed themselves into the Imelda Marcos of the streets, such was the trail of riches he was leaving in his sorry slipstream.

He stepped over another crack in the tiles, maintaining a balance with his arms outstretched like a high wire act. He was a high wire act in these days all right, and the safety net had been withdrawn for the intrigue of the paying crowd. His hands shook, his mechanism was almost gone. He had to now get back to his truck for two reasons. One was to get to his hand sanitizer. The other need was to urinate, and this he could only do at his parents' house, in the sanctuary of a bathroom he knew with soap he could touch.

Later that night, Marvin was scheduled to visit him in Brampton. Marvin the Healer was a kind man, and a reference from his friend, M_____. Marv was an expert in - and professor of – the study of addiction, and brought tolerance, energy and studied meditation. Marv would come eight times in total and seemed to really care. Joey got a lot from these sessions. Marv only charged fifty bucks including his travel costs and time, which only underlined his true and benevolent motive. This would be Marv's final visit for within twenty-four hours, Joey observed a fly in the bathroom. In the same room as his toothbrush, which had already been propped up and cordoned off from touching anything. The Joey that followed in the ensuing three days would make the switching deviant in the pharmacy, stepping over tile cracks and avoiding shades of red appear like the most judicious and calmly measured professional. He fell apart.

That fly shat on my damned toothbrush and scrunched it in with its toxic back legs. The horrible little monster. That isn't God's creation. It is an abomination. Its crowning glory in its pathetic life is to shit on my toothbrush. I cannot cope. Why should I even try to cope?

Ka-boooooom! KA-BOOOOOM!

'I am sorry, Marv. You are a good man. Thank you.'

Joey promised to continue to meditate. And it was *adios* to professional number five.

A new meltdown lasted for days, but the repercussions of the anxiety, depression, OCD and now phobias formed the core of his awful days. They determined his level of sadness, fogged up his vision, forced him to twitch every minute or so and made the simplest of tasks unreasonably heavy burdens.

One bright spot that fall was that his old pals at Woodbridge Strikers asked him to come back and coach some kids. He readily accepted, believing that the natural exuberance and genuine love of soccer from the youth would help to mask his terrors. He felt optimistic that he would be able to garner some real positivity from the experience. To approach the project in this frame of mind gave him real hope. There was no real dread, and so there were no real chinks in his armour as he headed back to familiar turf, coordinates that held truly beautiful memories. He allowed these warm feeling to wash over him, taking every ounce of spiritual strength from his recollections. It was as if he had paid into a pension and could now benefit from his investments.

Things started well. The kids were enthusiastic, and they all responded to Joey's natural affinity for the game and his transparently generous spirit. He was a pied piper of sorts and felt the reciprocated love from the kids. There was genuine talent, and he was reminded of his own trajectory. This might have led to the first crack in his defence, for that was the warm fall day that he thought he saw a Band Aid on the field, and he was then unable – physically and mentally – to go to that side of the field. (It was, in fact, some old orange peel.) He got home that day and threw his coach's uniform, first into the wash and then into the garbage. He then had to turn up to future training sessions in random clothing, something that first alerted the club elders to possible issues. They were paying him well, and rightly expected a minimum standard. They soon observed him with breathing difficulties, and then, unable to blow any whistle for fear of germs, would hold it in the air as far from his face as possible. The kids all knew by this stage but were remarkably accommodating and kind to him. It would have been so easy to mock him, kids being kids after all, and therein lies the high regard in which they all held him. The club – with deep regret - had to let him go, but boy was it a relief for him. And that was the night he was introduced – this time by his friend, Grace – to a pleasant old Greek lady (the seventh on the conveyor belt of promise land pioneers and long overdue saviours) who convinced Joey that they could fix him. Athena was a nice old lass, who believed in her discipline. She practised Bowen therapy at her home in North Toronto. This was a technique named after a mid-twentieth century Australian, Thomas Ambrose Bowen that stretches the soft tissue fascia, the ligaments, tendons and muscles, releasing pain points and rebooting the physique. She believed in it, because it had worked on dozens and hundreds of aching limbs and torsos over the years. But Joey was not a regular and uniform case. As Silvio would readily point out, it is somewhat tough to fix a problem under the hood of some vintage wheels if one cannot locate the issue. Diagnosis, diagnosis, diagnosis. The word is even a Greek one.

'Did you know that, Joey? Diagnosis, it comes from the Greek. *Gnosis,*' Athena told him.

- "scientific discrimination," especially in pathology, "the recognition of a disease from its symptoms," 1680s, medical Latin application of Greek diagnosis or gnosis "a discerning, distinguishing," from stem of diagignōskein "discern, distinguish," literally "to know thoroughly" or "know apart (from another)," from dia "between" ..

'I did not know *that*, Athena. Can you find one?'

'Well, let's have a look, shall we? But first, we can talk.'

And talk they did. The appointment was for one hour, but her empty-ish schedule, the lateness in the day and Athena's benevolent and caring approach that sought to find a solution for the poor boy meant that they spoke for two hours or more during which time, Joey wept and felt a true, albeit temporary release. The catharsis ('Another Greek word,' said Athena) revolved around Joey's guilt and anguish about having hurt that poor girl. He had truly loved her, but this love was transposed upon a wild, young, curious and somewhat lust-greedy personality. Utterly normal for a young man with Mediterranean blood. But this did not help The Girl, and so his tears poured like an open faucet. They gushed. They had been blocked and frozen, but now they flowed. He felt the mental pressure relent for the first time in months. If only they had stuck – and not boldly twisted - on sixteen…

'Ok, Joey, this is wonderful progress. I think we can now see what impact this all has on you physically. Would you lie down on the table, please? We try some Bowen…'

'Oh, yeah, I am not sure about that, thanks, Athena.'

'Oh! we must. We have made some real forward movement here. If we add to this some work on your tight muscles and tendons and tissue, you will sleep like a baby tonight and for weeks, this will be so. Please…' and she gestured to the raised medical massage table in the far corner of her plush suburban home.

'Can I ask you not to touch my head and neck, please, Athena?'

'Oh, please, trust me. We make you well together.'

And trust her he did, for the previous time (well over the allotted hour) had truly indicated her kindness and ability to source some of the issue. SOME of the issue. Not but all.

She worked on his arms and legs as he lay face down. She kneaded some sore points. She executed the procedure like a professional. She did not hurt him. But when he thought she was going near his neck, he panicked. Not from anything she did, just his own mental machinations.

He screamed. The adrenaline hit him. Lights flashed in his startled eyes.

Damn! Ohhh sweet Jesus! I can't breathe. I can't breaaaaathe.

He flipped from the table, crumpled and folded towards the sanctuary of the floor, a place from where he could fall no more, and therefore minimize the looming terror.

'I can't breathe, Athena. I caaaaannn'ttt brrreeeeaaathe.'

He struggled for breath, his vision blurred and faded around the edges of the screen, he was dizzy, and felt close to losing consciousness.

'Bite your finger, Joey. Bite your finger.'

This was a supposed method to deflect the attention and distract the brain with a decoy. His cerebral functions were broken, but he was not stupid. His brain recognised this horror, he had felt it previously, and so such techniques were flimsy and juvenile. Boys against men.

He was now in the fetal position on her floor, as she coaxed him and tried to offer a comfort that would bring him back from the edge.

✿

An hour later, he pulled up on the driveway of the family home, the returning and defeated army to the independent state ruled with benevolence by Silvio and Mary. The homeland. His parents were there outside the front of the house chatting with their neighbour.

He opened the car door and got out. He closed it, and semi-staggered towards the house. His eyes betrayed his mental state to Silvio, who for the first time, and perhaps through the embarrassment of such a sight in front of the other lady, veered towards a flustered anger.

Oh god no. Now he is angry with me. I cannot take much more of this. This has to be the bottom. This HAS to be the bottom.

Nope, the phone call in November 2009 would show Joey that it was nowhere near the bottom. He had merely landed on a massive sinkhole that was about to give way into a nether world of utter misery.

KA-BOOM! KA-BOOOOOM! KA-BOOOOOOOOOOM!

✿

Mary answered the phone. Everything was normal. From the sofa, Joey heard the cadence and tone and rhythm of the one-sided, horror-laden conversation. It resembled the calls we have all heard on the television a thousand times, and secretly and silently dread and fear the time it comes to us. The pauses, the rise of pitch in fear with many questions desperately trying to come out. The scream.

'Noooooo!'

The tears.

The gulps.

The sobs. The breathlessness. The primordial and bestial yelps. The Nat Geo documentary on the plains of the Kalahari has shown us the brutal unforgiving side of nature. And death. Unavoidable death.

Nonna had six to nine months left, as the creeping vicious twins of cancer and dementia made a pincer movement on Joey's favourite person in the whole world, his grandma, Angela. Nature is cruel, but also oddly forgiving at the most perverse of times, for the dementia allowed this stately lady to be largely unaware of her other ailment, the one that would soon extinguish the most precious light of all.

Joey was now working silly hours at a gym chain, The Fitness Place. He was selling personal training, audaciously, prodigiously, prolifically and in the ballsy sand-to-the-Arabs style he had honed at the time share gig. His day off was Wednesday, and this was his favourite day of the week. It was the day he got to visit his grandparents,

Antonio and Angela. They lived forty minutes away. His journey there never failed to enthuse him and to lift his flagging spirits. This was the farthest he could venture from the family stead. It was an extension of Silvio's independent state, an enclave of safety and security. Here they obeyed the same flag and enjoyed an unspoken and familial bond. Literally unspoken, for Angela spoke no words of English, her grandson supremely monolinguistic. This only elevated their bond, for they needed nothing as piffling as words. That lioness does not need words to express herself and, barring an odd growl and tooth-showing, nature understands that there is nothing greater than her love for her young. So, it was with Angela, *Nonna,* and her Joey. From baby to toddler to youth to man theirs was a special connection. They would sit and hold hands. Eye contact and kisses on her cheek or on his was comfortingly adequate. This was a preternatural bond. Trifling words be damned. Antonio could translate into something north of pidgin English, but they understood each other telepathically.

Upon his arrival, even if it were at midnight or nine a.m., her enquiry had always been the same.

'*Che stai a mangia?*' 'What did you eat today?' as she rose to head to the kitchen to nourish her young.

But now, he was lucky if she recognized him.

I could really do with you right now, Nonna. I need your help.

She stared past him and asked her adoring husband if he had come over to see her today (across the Italian countryside of the 1930s) on his horse.

'Sei venuto da me sul tuo cavallo oggi, tesoro?'

The heartbreaking beauty and unabashed romance within this one line is enough to push the sturdiest of us to gulp back a tear, as we ponder the remarkable world of love and time.

He was outselling everyone in the gym. His numbers were phenomenal. But if he picked up a weight, he would feel dizzy and nauseous.

There was something happening in him, and he pondered again

the Las Vegas mirage. He could not tell if what he saw on the horizon was real. He staggered across a proverbial desert, parched and confused.

Is that an oasis on the lip of the sand dune? Is that my salvation? I can only be cured when I know what is wrong.

They promoted him from assistant manager to manager. The money was good, and perhaps he would have stayed and endured the psychological terror had it not been for the fight. For the spilling of blood.

Two customers got into a brawl that resembled two stags butting each other. Even though it happened in the foyer of the building, Joey's colleague, a lovely chap called Yad, had broken it up and trailed rhesus negative scarlet all the way through the gym and into the offices and the changing rooms.

The building tensions with the vice president, John then were elevated as Joey's blood phobia seeped into every minute of his day. It came to a head the day John insisted that Joey shave.

'You cannot sell a thing with that scruff on your face.'

'Watch me.'

'If I don't have a signed contract for some personal training on my desk this morning, you are going home to shave.'

'Yes, John.'

The other guys in the gym were all the clean-shaven and jacked types. They were perpetually confused by his success, but they had no idea of his past in sales. He was posting $45,000 in sales every two weeks. He was the best salesperson across all of Canada.

And so, he returned to John's office within two hours with a signed deal. He delivered it while stroking the fuzz on his chin and cheeks. It was a major *screw-you* to John.

And if one is going, leave the party early. On a high note. He sidestepped the rouge trails, and he was gone. *Adios, muchachos!*

And like THAT, he was on the road to Keele and Wilson and that small bungalow with the live-in help now, where he sought and nestled into his sanctuary with a fine old lady in her final weeks.

She still smelled as angelic and as perfect as ever as her physical frame faded with her mind. What she never lost until the final hours was the mischievous and otherworldly laugh and gloriously arc'd sense of humour.

Still, she called him Govi (pronounced *Jo'vee*) and chuckled inwardly as she did. He recalled the hours they'd spent together driving with Antonio to his boyhood soccer games. He recalled the heart attack she had suffered in 1990 but had recovered like the steel factory worker she had once been.

They made them tough.

They made them beautiful.

By gad, they broke the mould.

And when she was laid to rest, he smiled through the gushing tears, when he dredged up her words.

'*Sei venuto da me sul tuo cavallo oggi, tesoro?*'

Did you come to me on your horse today, darling?

The pre-eminent Italian countryside would never be the same again. Those days were gone.

"Now cracks a noble heart. Good-night, sweet princess,
And flight of angels sing thee to thy rest."

Chapter 13

'YOU ARE FINE,' THEY SAID.

He had arranged to be at her house at seven. She was beautiful. Ordinarily he would have asked her to come to his basement, but gorgeousness of this elevated and lofty level demanded that the mountain move to Mohammed.

He left home in time and hopped into his jeep, enthused by the thought of the face and body that awaited him. He stepped over the cracks in the pavement, tiptoeing like the Pink Panther, agile and aware.

But there was something more to this. Something he had not thought through.

Fifteen minutes later, he pulled up on her driveway. He got out of the driver's side, scanned the icy ground for splatters of red. A shoulder twitched. An eye tic'd. He looked up to see the vision of beauty, framed by the soft butter yellow of the hallway lamp. The silhouette he saw initially gave way to his seeing the contours of her remarkable face as he neared, and the dark shape became facial features. Her mouth was agape, her eyes wide open, and her hand raised to her forehead. She staggered backwards in shock.

'Joey! JOEY!'

'Y-y-y-y-es?'

'What on earth…?'

'W-w-w-hat?'

Oh Christ, what did I do?

'WHAT ARE YOU DOING?' she said. She may have held back a small giggle.

She pointed down to his feet then her hand raised slowly to indicate the rest of his legs and torso.

'What are you wearing?' and finally she burst out laughing.

Joey looked down at his black dress shoes with no laces, his sport socks over his track pants so that they would not touch the ground and a leather jacket. He looked like some half-baked Albanian hitman, trying to fit in, straight off the boat. Poor Joey Tomaselli. The thing was, he was still invited in. he brushed it off with humour, the same mischievous and adorable glint in the eye that allowed him to avoid burdensome tasks and duties in second grade. He had ploughed this furrow previously. Make them smile. It'll all be all right.

And at least, he was still getting out. He had not given up. He had retrenched and regressed, but the struggle continued. He sensed the Nevada desert mirage. One day, there would an oasis, full of clean, fresh water to quench his parched mind. For now, he still sensed that he had trodden in more than he could chew.

And so later that evening something happened that most of us, the chap in the street, would rate as horrific and to be avoided at all costs, but there was something in the car crash that Joey was about to instigate - though quite accidentally- that he, viscerally in his gut, felt might have some kind of upside to it. Of late, he had seen the world through a half-empty glass, every silver lining having the most obsidian and threatening cloud. But oddly here, as he drove his old red (yes, red) BMW two-door three series into the back of a stationary car, something told him that an opportunity was at hand.

It was nighttime on November the eighth, 2009, around nine. He was talking to his friend, Sandra on the phone when he collided into the back of the other vehicle, a RAV4 on that Brampton side street.

Joey smashed his head on the ceiling of the car up by the door. The bump had thrust him high off his seat. He was going close to seventy kilometres per hour. He did not see stars and was not unconscious for a split second. The other driver got out of his car and approached the BMW. Joey lobbed his phone onto the passenger-side floor.

The middle-aged man held out his hands, 'I'm ok. Are you ok?'

He was immediately conciliatory and concerned for the obvious offender.

Joey lifted his hands.

'Yeah, yeah. I am fine. I am so sorry!'

Joey opened his door and stepped out gingerly.

'Let me get my insurance documents. And do you have a phone? Take my number. I will pay for everything.'

'OK, no rush.'

Through all of this, Joey realised he was going to benefit from this. Such clarity. Such instinct.

Hospital. Hospital. Get myself to a hospital. Maybe they can find what's wrong with me. Yes! Hospital!

Five minutes later, he was trundling the damaged car onto the driveway at home. He went in, did not see Silvio and Mary, and did not search them out. Instead, he unhooked her car keys from their home, and swiftly slipped back out of the door. He reversed out slowly and carefully, swung the wheel, and then slipped it into drive. Ten minutes later, he was in the car park at of a nearby hospital.

He went into the A&E, where he was about to embark on a seven-hour wait to be seen. He was fooled into thinking the wait would not be too long, but there was a mirage here too. The old trick where they call you into a room – a *Waiting for Godot* purgatory, halfway house to hell – and lure you into thinking this wait is not so bad.

For most of the seven hours, Joey stood in the middle of the room to avoid sinks, worktops and seats where the likelihood of spilled blood was, in his puddled mind, that much greater.

Eventually, Joey had a CAT scan. Joey's gut feeling at the scene of the accident was possibly correct, for the keen-eyed doctor saw something but was unable to confirm or communicate to Joey what it was.

'I know there's something wrong with me, doctor. Please help me.'

'Look, Joey. The good news is that I can get you an MRI a week from today! How is that?'

'Thanks, doctor,' he replied.

'Come back here on the sixteenth. At 10 a.m. The MRI is nothing to worry about. It can tell us so much about your body. Are you sure you feel all right to drive home?'

'I do. I feel better now after what you have told me.'

'Good. Drive carefully. Take care.'

And like that, he was off into the night again, stepping over the cracks in the hospital tiles with the agility of the former soccer player in him, hopping over slide tackles and moving in on goal. It felt good to take something shit and transform it into hope. He was so used to the opposite. Was he mounting some late-stage comeback?

This is it, Joey. They're going to be able to tell me why I am like this.

He drove home, parked and then walked from his car. In the early morning light, he was shocked to see how full his back seat was with new shoeboxes. He had only cleared it out the week before.

Oh, god. Maybe I am getting worse? They will cure me. They will tell me what's wrong. I know it. Oh! glorious car crash.

The thought of forty-five minutes in an MRI is enough to send the sanest guy into a small frenzy. The human being is not designed to cope with such a claustrophobic experience. It is like being buried alive. The brain plays tricks, we are fine in our repose on a bed or a sofa, still and chilled. But in the tube, we hit the panic button to be extracted. And there we are, back at the beginning having to start again. So, for someone of Joey's mental fragility at the stage, he did remarkably well to remain as still as the doctors required for the full forty-five minutes.

There is salvation ahead. For that, I can do anything. For that, you can do anything, Joey, he told himself.

The power of the mind is a remarkable thing. His determination to do this the first time might yet be a microcosm of Joey's story. It was perhaps the same determination that took him to quacks and hypnotists and therapists. What if the treatment he was being offered was the one to save him? The answer had to be out there.

You can do this, Joey. Push forward. Tira Avanti.

A pretty nurse said to him, 'Your family doctor will be in touch.'

'How long?' he asked.

'Not too long,' she said. 'Hard to say.'

'OK, thank you.'

The call came within three days. It was from the usual receptionist at Dr. Brian's office.

'We have a referral for you, Joey. To see a neurologist. It is one month from now. I will email you the details.'

'Excellent,' Joey said. 'Thank you.'

He was genuinely excited.

They have to find something. I am making progress, at last.

Mary drove him there that day. Perhaps she sensed the excitement within him, and therefore the potential disappointment. She also remembered the car crash.

They met with the neurologist, a seasoned doctor with a wise way about him.

'You appear to be fine,' he announced while examining the imaging. 'I have seen cases similar to this, where the best cure is to be active,' he shrugged. 'Are you able to lift weights?'

'I feel pain when I work out. I feel dizzy when I lift weights. Working out is killing me.'

'Ok, I see. Well, at least you are young. This is truly puzzling...'

✧

On the way out, he skipped over the tile cracks on the way back out to the street.

✧

And so, in July of 2010, Joey procured a CD of the MRI...

Wise boy, clever move, instinctive and instinctual move.

And off he went for a second opinion with his supposed evidence in his hands.

A young Greek doctor simply concurred with the first neurologist, that whatever was wrong with him was not immediately evident.

Joey was zigzagging between accepted medical paths and the more unorthodox options. The next one was a lady who had appeared on Oprah. She was a therapist with a book published to many plaudits, and she now competed with professionals, who had diplomas, Doctorates and Hippocratic* Oaths, framed and adorning the disinfected walls, competed to source Joey's ailment.

> I swear by Apollo Healer by Asclepius by <u>Hygieia</u>, by Panacea and by all the gods and goddesses, making them my witnesses, that I will carry out, according to my ability and judgment, this oath and this indenture.
>
> To hold my teacher in this art equal to my own parents; to make him partner in my livelihood; when he is in need of money to share mine with him;

---

* God, not another Greek!, he chuckled to himself, for he loved them really.

to consider his family as my own brothers, and to teach them this art, if they want to learn it, without fee or indenture; to impart precept, oral instruction, and all other instruction to my own sons, the sons of my teacher, and to indentured pupils who have taken the Healer's oath, but to nobody else.

Every doctor swore this oath, this promise, to protect and heal with utmost benevolence and verve. They had to.

She showed him the cutting from her appearance with Oprah. *Maybe she is the one?*

I will use those dietary regimens which will benefit my patients according to my greatest ability and judgment, and I will do no harm or injustice to them.[7] Neither will I administer a poison to anybody when asked to do so, nor will I suggest such a course. Similarly, I will not give to a woman a pessary to cause abortion. But I will keep pure and holy both my life and my art. I will not use the knife, not even, verily, on sufferers from stone, but I will give place to such as are craftsmen therein.

Into whatsoever houses I enter, I will enter to help the sick, and I will abstain from all intentional wrong-doing and harm, especially from abusing the bodies of man or woman, bond or free. And whatsoever I shall see or hear in the course of my profession, as well as outside my profession in my intercourse with men, if it be what should not be published abroad, I will never divulge, holding such things to be holy secrets.

He held his legs off the carpet away from a dubious dark stain in her consulting room. Oprah pictures here and there. This latest one

176

suggested medication and two years in a clinic. She could get him in there.

'I have to go. Thank you for your time. Here is your two hundred.'

He was about to spend his thirtieth birthday, crying in his basement. He had always pictured his thirtieth in Las Vegas, having the time of his life. The Nevada mirage remained. Mirages can be devilish fiends. It is what they do.

> Now if I carry out this oath, and break it not, may
> I gain for ever reputation among all men for my
> life and for my art; but if I break it and forswear
> myself, may the opposite befall me

Oh God. Give me more doctors in this vein. Without them, I know I will soon take my own life.

'When you don't look, you hurt people and that's not fair. WHEN YOU DO NOT LOOK, YOU HURT PEOPLE, AND THAT IS NOT FAIR'

These are the words of Doctor Daniel Amen, a Lebanese psychiatrist living in the United States. Despite the latest professional's advice to come off social media, Joey stayed on Facebook and continued to text his friends. He was scrolling through one night after the latest disaster, when he stumbled across a site called *Illumeably*. Perhaps the algorithm had sought him out from his searches. There was a You Tube video of six minutes and fifty-seven seconds. It was called *What a Psychiatrist Learned from 87,000 Brain Scans*.

Joey watched. And then watched again. He had no idea if there was any relevance to his case, but had that same gut feeling about the mirage in the desert.

The eloquent, funny, and benevolent doctor is on stage giving a talk to his peers. He is dressed neatly in a brown-grey suit, an informal black round-necked tee-shirt beneath and with an earpiece and a mic. His hair is thin, his features small, and he uses his hands to annunciate. We like him.

He begins to speak about his godson and his nephew in California, Andy. Andy is a sweet and tender boy of nine, who, he discovers in a chat with the boy's mother, has just physically attacked a girl in his class. They have found art in Andy's room, where he has hanged himself from a tree.

The boy's mother takes him to the doctor, the uncle, the god-father – this same Daniel Amen. He urges the boy has a brain scan, where they find the boy's left temporal lobe has been almost completely invaded by a tumour and a cyst. Despite some medical resistance to connect the suicidal and murderous thoughts of a boy barely out of short trousers to the insidious ailment, Doctor Amen *(Amen, how apt)* finds a famous surgeon at UCLA who will operate. He does so successfully, and Andy smiles for the first time in a year.

Joey weeps. He is unsure why precisely.

'When you don't look, you hurt people and that's not fair. WHEN YOU DO NOT LOOK, YOU HURT PEOPLE, AND THAT IS NOT FAIR'

It was now a race between hope and despair.

It was now a race for Joey Tomaselli between an answer and his parents receiving that dreadful knock, and being told, 'Yes, I am so sorry, he *did* leave a note.'

WHEN YOU DO NOT LOOK, YOU HURT PEOPLE, AND THAT IS NOT FAIR'

Chapter 14

J oey was only in reality half-way through the conveyor belt of
saviours. If he had known this, he may have ended it all then.
Is ignorance bliss? Orson Welles once spoke about *Citizen Kane*,
and how he had only made a classic because he had not known the
rules of filmmaking. He called it the Confidence of Ignorance. There
is much to be said in favour of being unaware.

And now he was back in the mall, avoiding cracks between – and
the slightest molecule of red - on the tiles. One moment he resembled
a triple-jumper as he leapt over an awkward combination of flooring.
The next he was more American Gladiator, hugging the walls to cir-
cumnavigate a dubious hue. Then Donkey Kong, leaping in the air.
He was his own demented video game. No wonder everyone seemed
to be whispering and texting and discussing how Joey Tomaselli had
finally lost it. Even when he sat with friends, he thrust his head from
side to side from the crescendo of pain and confusion. They joked
privately that he was Stevie Wonder.

He now stood over a spot of red – it was a sliver of paper from a
sachet of white sugar - in a coffee shop, trying to stick his ostrich head
down to the imaginary sand. He stayed there for ten minutes, maybe
more. Concerned customers edged around him, as the manager whis-
pered to her staff. They eyed him suspiciously every few seconds.

He was on his way to see a naturopath, another – the eleventh - who had told him, 'Yes, I can help you.'

This guy – a well-meaning sort, who Joey was sure had helped many others – reeled off a list of natural remedies, botanical supplements, and Chinese herbs. Dandelion leaf, St. John's wort, St, Francis; wort, homeopathic remedies, black cohosh, echinacea, feverfew, evening primrose, ginseng, gingko biloba, saw palmetto, hawthorn, goldenseal, goat's rue, magnesium bisglycinate, quercetin, willow herb, black tea and vitamins B12, D, E, B, and A.

Joey took one of each and gave him a credit card that was charged $800 for the rattling sack load. He felt kind of nervous buying them, unsure at the time as to why. It became clear later in his room with a large glass of water. He could not put any of them near his mouth. The next day, he tossed the lot.

One might have thought this would have dissuaded him from the visit to professional number twelve, a nutritionist. He was ticking them off at a fair old rate now. Not that a nutritionist doesn't have sagacity and wisdom about the body, but one should never take a knife to a gun fight. It cost $500. No processed foods, only natural sugars in fruit, take it easy on the chocolate and candy bars. Manuka honey, fruit, vegetables, grains, nuts, fresh fish were all great cornerstones.

Later that night, he called The Girl again to tell her about *Nonna*. Again, she picked up first time. Again, it was a truly abysmal idea.

I'm in a basement. She's working in the hottest club in town. Muzik.

He wished her well, but all of this just underlined the gradient of his decline.

You're a selfish fool, Joey Tomaselli, he thought. What did you expect her to say? Of course, she was sad about Nonna. Of course, this is my problem now. It would have been a problem shared had we been together. And I am the reason we are not. You make no sense sometimes, he thought.

It was cordial, as was the farewell. But it achieved little.

He picked up the sheets of his diet plan.

He felt sad. This was his life now.

Well for the next three months until he decided, 'No more!' The pain would not subside.

Hello chocolate, my old friend.

In the limo dressed in black, Joey thought back to Nonna's final days.

I miss you so much.

He wondered how long she might have lived had she not fallen going into the house that day. They had said she had six to nine months to live. She had already barrelled through that and was fully mobile after ten. Her fall had taken her backwards, and she had cracked the back of her skull.

Joey had got the call, and so desperate was he to see her that he had donned some 'toxic' old shoes in order to rush to her side. It was tough, but he rose to the occasion. Anything for her. Now he took a gun to a knife fight. The phobia was beaten in these moments.

You see, you CAN do it, he told himself.

Silvio was there when he arrived, Mary was on her way.

Nonna was face down on her bed, so that they could access the injury. There was blood, but again Joey prevailed. He was in no mood to back down. She knew it was he. He held her hand. He wiped her forehead and pushed her hair back from her angelic face. What was she thinking of? Her days as a girl in Italy? The tiniest of memories? The precise smell of the bakeries on summer mornings with seventy years still to relish? A shady corner in the summer? The stars? The Mediterranean mistral shaking off the leaves in fall? Christmas presents from her own *papi* and his war stories? Her early days with her horseman? Their first kiss on the cobbles? The days when she gave birth and changed diapers? Saw them all grow? Days turned to years. Sobbed at their weddings? Or breathed grateful rapture and well-informed and instinctual euphoria at the arrival of her grandchildren? Did her memory stray to her own schooldays? Her own mother? How she now knew how they felt as she herself stared into the abyss of eternity? Was she able to extract the beauty of her own life over and above the requirement to say *arrivederci?* We will never know, but her eyes did broadcast an urging and a deep love to her precious *Govi.*

Did she know the news that Joey was now told? That her Antonio, her mounted hero on horseback, now had stomach cancer. If she did, her dementia would have robbed her of this malevolent and malicious knowledge for large chunks of her waken days. Ah the *Confidence of Ignorance* again. Nature can also deal a benevolent hand in between such unforgiving bouts of viciousness.

They would treat him with chemotherapy, but it was not early in its keen-to-metastasize progress. It was stage three. It was bleak.

The fall had happened on the Monday. When Govi arrived on the Tuesday, Nonna was on her back and hooked up to machines that only told one inevitable story with the most inevitable ends so imminent.

'I am sorry, Joey. The decline has been quite sudden,' said the kind nurse.

The scream that the boy let pass his lips might have disturbed those at the farthest reaches of the building well-accustomed to solar plexus bellows of utter sadness, as souls fell away, and all we are left with are memories of holding loved ones. Like smoke to hold. Gone. And old black and white pictures on the dresser. No amount of yelling will ever bring them back. Celebrating their life in their absence always a poor second to just ten more minutes with them, in our urgent grasp.

Again, he wiped her forehead, pushed back her hair, and allowed her to know he was there.

We do not need words anyway. Never did. We are above that, aren't we?

They truly did transcend our lowly forms of communication. Just words. Piffling words.

Again, he vanquished his phobia for these crucial moments. In this, he took nuggets of hope. Was this her parting gift? An ability to stand firm against his tormenting illnesses.

At one a.m. that next morning, Mary and his sister, Sandra convinced him to go home and sleep. He relented, on the condition that he would take up his willing and most-decent vigil in the morning. Just twenty minutes after he left, the great lady passed.

He thought of all of this, as he rode in the limo to the funeral. His grandfather's.

Nonno had passed just six months after his bride.

Joey recalled the limo ride to Nonna's funeral, and he remembered how he had dreaded the drive with someone else in control of his destiny – at the wheel. This is not how he did things. He felt powerless and exposed. How he shook and sweated and twitched as the long line of relatives paid their respects Italian-style. Yes, it had been a beautiful and dignified tribute to Angela. Of course, it had. How he had begged for the OCD to leave him for the day, how he tried to channel her strength for this and for one last time. He had been able to overcome it for the brief moments in the hospital, as her fading eyes had encouraged him. But with her that bit more distant and no longer alive, it seemed that the potency of her love no longer powered him.

You're on your own now, Joey, he thought.

✿

Joey had now noticed a change in Mary. One that he completely understood. She was losing both of her parents.

You need to get a grip for others now, he told himself. You have leaned on them long enough.

He remembered the time he turned the car crash into something positive. He still had the CD of the MRI. He told himself now that he would need to be more self-reliant for the sake of his poor mother. Alchemy. To turn something bad into something golden. There was only so much she can do. *That* was the day she sent him to visit Nonno.

✿

The words of a Welshman's famous death poem are heard, and we shall discover more of this soon. Rage! Rage!

He pulled up at the small house, and up there on the balcony was an old man, staring off into the distance. He did not seem to see Joey arrive. He knew what was coming next. This was the first time in sixty-two years he had been without her. Since he was a teenager in riding boots, dashing and handsome and not a thought of what he would be doing in six decades time on the other side of the world.

Joey visited every week until the time he was moved into the hospital. The day before he passed, Joey and he had a remarkable talk. It lasted for hours, and it was notable for the clarity of Nonno's English. What a pep talk he gave, like a final scene in a movie just when you think it is all too late. And he ate well that day, something he had not done for months with the marauding tumour causing havoc in his gut and beyond. There are anecdotes of strange wells of strength and life being tapped into just before the ultimate fall into death, marble cold and still death. Nonno's display was one last hurrah. Joey would regret forever how he did not kiss his grandfather goodbye because of a drop of blood on his sheets. Well, tomorrow would be too late. And therein is a lesson that billions of us could heed.

Poetic words of meteors across the bay, and green lights at the point of death.

Time to get in the saddle of your horse, Antonio. One last ride. Go find that fair maiden who defines you. She waits for you, you know. Now gallop to her. Not a second to lose, my friend.

And like *that,* he was gone.

✿

Joey would see them again. Nonna three times in dreams. Nonno just once.

Each time, he knew she was dead and that it was a dream. He still welcomed her with every ounce of his soul. Grateful and aware.

The first time she gave him a letter. Dream analysis would suggest that this revolved around their unorthodox but supremely solid communication. The note read, 'Joey, I know what you're going through. Keep going. God is always watching you.'

Tira avanti. Push forward.

The *I* in the note was adorned with a prune of all things. It seemed so bizarre to him that this was a key element of what he would always recall. A prune?

Dream analysis suggests two things here. Both are unerringly accurate. The prune represents a need to get rid of old habits; to clear out the constipated bowel of life. To rid oneself of old crap. To unblock the emotions. It also represents ageing, and here she was, his old nonna was visiting him. The brain is the most marvellous muscle.

In his second dream, Nonna and Govi walked around the block near his house, as he had done in his darkest moments. This was her – and his – way of telling him(self) that she was always with him in his darkest moments, and she would be in the future, if he ever thought of her. He wept and sobbed.

Nonna's third nocturnal appearance and her curtain call came in the middle of a crowded room. 'I cannot keep coming to you. I have to go to the others,' she told him in English. She appeared as a fifty-year-old, pristine, regal, noble, august and in her pomp still. He again cried, knowing *this* was it.

Nonno's single visit contained a portent, an omen. He appeared with a stroller. The stroller held a baby boy. His granddaughter and Joey's sister, Nadia had been trying to become a mother for years, so far in vain. And it was because of these unsuccessful times for her and the barren time she seemed destined to experience that he brushed off the likelihood of a pregnancy.

He was spending more time at Sandra's. She had two children of her own, Nicholas and Cassandra, and Joey loved to hang out with them. They were ten and six, and like at Woodbridge, the children naturally gravitated towards the pied piper. He purposefully spent time there with them to mitigate and minimise the growing physical and mental anguish, the depths of which he was now plumbing. But his head and body hurt. Throbbed relentlessly. It was like a perpetual and perennial hangover without the fun part of the booze and the party. He felt like he had been hit by a Mac truck.

I cannot do this anymore. I might just end this.

It was the first night of Sandra's vacation when he was house-sitting. The perfect opportunity to take his own life.

No one to disturb me.

No chance of being found and their saying it was a call for help.

There was a knock on the door. He almost ignored it, but instead he shuffled to answer it.

'Nadia! What is it?'

She looked up and she had tears rolling down her face.

'Joey. I am pregnant! I am going to have a baby!'

He thought of his grandfather, rolled his head back – and despite the pain – yelled a scream to the night stars, the same ones that were also now shining on that ancient Italian hillside just before dawn of a new day, on that old bakery, the unchanged town square, the cobbled stones that had witnessed their first kiss, next to a snorting stallion, who scratched and tapped at the ground, seemingly offering his tough-to-earn approval at the preternatural strength of the vast love at hand - far, far away and long, long ago.

Chapter 15

He said he liked her bracelet, and could he have a look, please? Really, he just wanted to look at her hands. Was she clean? Was that a small nick near her fingernail?

He was running out of clothes. Despite two dozen empty shoe boxes in the back of his car, he had no shoes to wear. He walked to his car in his socks, even in December.

I need those boxes in there. Ever since that back seat got a drop of blood in it. My car is now a two-seater. Or it is may as well be. That back-seat is dead to me. I have a better chance of walking into the United States without a passport than I do of invading the space in the back of my own vehicle, he thought.

He remembered the previous evening and how he had spent an hour in the restaurant bathroom with his hands in the air, waiting for someone to open the door to liberate him.

That was insane, he told himself. I won't even be able to hold the baby. Uncle Joey is a joke. A sad, pathetic joke of a human being.

He thought of the new girl he had met, and how disturbed she had been when they had made love and he spent the next three hours in the shower.

My fluids are toxic, he told himself several times a time. Dexter and his blood spatters have nothing on me. I should have done his job.

It was a mild miracle she had hopped with gusto into his bed after he had made her cover her hands and arms in hand sanitizer in the front seat of the jeep.

'I wish I could take you out,' he had told her. 'I am not right.' 'Perhaps you deserve someone who can treat you right. It is going to be really hard for you to be with me.'

He was getting no better. And the toll on Mary from her parents' passing was intense. Mary took a cleaning job, many days on autopilot, glazed over. She had told her daughters to look after Joey if anything ever happened to her, and she was resigned now to Joey's condition being a permanent state. Her poker face never broadcast this to Joey. They at least spent many hours together, watching old movies in the afternoons before he made some vain attempts to venture out in the early evening. He almost always gave up before he reached the front door, slumping down in the living room, and gaping at the television set instead. He was exhausted of the standard and rehearsed answers he would have to give when friends and family asked how he was. He may as well have printed it out on a flier as a press release. He was so desperate he tried prescription glasses, even though he did not need them. Another Vegas mirage, and no watering hole. No salvation. 'More money down the drain,' moaned Silvio.

But if he thought he had hit rock bottom, then he was mistaken. Suicide beckoned. It takes some doing. They call it a coward's way out, but how on earth is anyone able to judge the mental anguish it takes to take one's own life? To call it a coward's way out is more than a cliché, it is mean and uninformed. By definition. For anyone who knows the truth is no longer here. Those who may have tried it unsuccessfully, are likely to be those who cried for help, knowing they'd be found in time. We hear about the strange plateau suicide cases find before the final act, an acceptance and a bizarre release from the pressure. The decision is made. This only goes to make the saddest news a greater shock to loved ones. 'He was fine. He was in good form. It must have been an accident.' Nope, this was a mirage. He was fine because he knew he now had an escape. It is also apparently tough to achieve the first time. Sometimes it takes a

few dry runs, like tipping a vending machine. Poor boy. Poor Joey.
He had made up his mind.

☼

He could hear the old guy working out in the garden. The astonishing smell of cut grass passed him on small rafts, intruders through
the open doors and windows. The remarkable tang from the lawn
was sweeter than ever before; a concentrated beauty like the sheer
whiteness of blossom described by palliative cancer patients fading in
the spring. There was a good reason his senses were on alert, and this
shall soon be explained. The gardener had liberated this aroma as he
struck down thousands of blades of young grass. In their prime. He
grafted out there in his spare time, powered by a source of energy that
compelled him to work, made him happiest when he was working,
and pushed on by a desire to keep working, to make things as beautiful for his family as he possibly could.

*"I could never work as hard as my father did for us but if only, IF ONLY,
he knew how hard I had worked not to give up. To not end it all. To not kill
myself," Joey thought.*

For every engine his old man sorted out and every buttercup or
tulip that thrived and wilted within his boundaries, it was perhaps
just a moment that he did not therefore have on his hands to tell his
son that he loved him. But Joey knew this, for he had also seen his
own personal National Geographic documentary on that fine species,
the Italian male.

So, it was all the more astonishing when Silvio marched in that
day, sweat on his brow, and came to his only son, lowered himself to
his haunches and to eye level with his boy. He fixed his gaze upon
him as if he sensed to perfection what was required.

His hand touched Joey, and he spoke.

"Come on, buddy."

And in the remaining few seconds before the magic wore off,
the old mechanic fixed everything in the world of his only boy.
The boy then knew his suicidal actions would only hurt beyond

comprehension this small nation state of Silvio and Mary the most. And the Italians are nothing if not patriotic.

"I don't like seeing you like this," he said.

And he paused, stood, and went back to tending his western border. It was the act of a true leader.

So, this is where we joined the tale of Joey Tomaselli. On a rapid decline.

Silvio's kindness brought him back the edge that day, but the vending machine had started to rock. And what happened next was a major muscular and jacked athlete shove on it, trying to floor it, and in doing so, bring down, lay low and then bury the tormented boy. He still thought of a resting place next to Nonna. The torment was just postponed.

Would she forgive me? he thought.

It was September 2011, and the family were away in Italy. Joey had a pal staying with him at the house. Matt was keeping an eye on him, though Joey was trying to maintain a semblance of normality with some prolific dating. No one would have guessed he was so close to the edge. Matt was cooking breakfast, as Joey showered. It was then he noticed something as he washed his nethers. Was this a scratch from a feisty lover?

Oh god, what's wrong with me now? Pain, anxiety, depression, phobias, OCD and now a sexually transmitted disease? I swear if this is true, I will not last the day. I don't even care how I do it.

He booked in to see his family doctor immediately. There was an opening that afternoon.

'You may have herpes,' the doctor said.

Ka-boooooom! Ka-booooooooom! KA-BOOOOOOOM!

He was close to blacking out.

'Yeah. I am pretty sure it could be herpes.' Let's get you to the clinic.

KA-BOOOOOOOOOOOOOOOM!

He did not remember driving home. The next thing he knew he was on the computer, looking up how herpes can make you 'shed' your skin. Well, Joey thought *this* referred to him, even though his phobias meant he did not dry himself properly and so he suffered from dry skin. He went down a rabbit hole online, convincing himself he had sore calves, another symptom of herpes.

I will kill myself. It is decided. First, I must call on the girls I have kissed and slept with. It is only fair.

He planned to do it that night and he sat as the kitchen table, ashen-faced, considering how best to execute himself. He had forgotten that was the night the family were arriving back from the old country.

According to the Centers for Disease Control and Prevention (CDC), more than one in six people in the United States between the ages of fourteen and forty-nine years have genital herpes.

The World Health Organization (WHO) say that globally, about sixty-seven per cent of people below the age of 50 years (which equates to three point seven billion people) have HSV-1. This is the virus that most often causes oral herpes.

According to the WHO, HSV-2 is more common in women; it affected 267 million women and 150 million men in 2012. This difference is due to the fact that women tend to contract HSV-2 more easily from sexual contact. (Medical News Today)

'Nice to meet you, Doctor L_____,' he said. Of course, he could not shake her hand. She touched diseased genitals for a living. It was a minor miracle he was even in these four walls.

'Nice to meet you too, Joey. Come on in.'

'Thank you.'

Joey told her of his ailments, and before he had reached the end of the sorrowful list, he stood up from his seat, turned and kicked a wall as hard as he ever kicked a soccer ball.

'Oh my,' she said. 'Please sit down, and let's talk.'

'There's nothing to discuss. I am finished. I cannot take this anymore.'

Tonight is the night. I am sorry, Mom. I am so sorry.

'Well at least let me see it.'

After all those he had consulted in this journey, it would have been insane for him to refuse to drop his flies. But he considered just that he was done. He had no energy left for his search. This was the final ignominy. The final kick in the teeth.

'Please. P-l-ease,' Doctor L_____ urged.

Had it not been for her kind manner and desire to live by that Oath of kindness and care, Joey would have been dead by midnight. *Les jeux sont faits.* Done deal.

You're here, Joey, he told himself. Drop your pants. Then you can slice your wrist or take the pills or go in front of the train in all good conscience. Just drop your pants, man.

One last task. *This* he could do. Just.

He did as she asked, as she pulled on two rubber gloves and pulled a lamp towards his exposed groin.

'Joey, this is NOT herpes. This is a scratch. I am happy to put my professional reputation on the line here. You have nothing to worry about. We can do an easy test and have the results back in seven to ten days.'

It was still fifty-fifty in his mind – a binary yes or no – but he should have heeded her determined words about her professional wisdom. That night (and perhaps) from a lofty height, a truly perverse god threw Joey Tomaselli a bone. He took it. He did not kill himself.

✧

Doctor L_____ was right. It was not herpes, and Joey was grateful that he had listened to this one. It may have been the reason he saw a third therapist, a fourteenth person. Doctor P_____ cut her prices out of sympathy, and one might presume from a confidence that she might do some good. Joey's pain was now cranked up to an almost perpetual eight out of ten. He saw her for three months.

'I so want to help you, Joey.'

She held eye contact, that simplest route to let some poor soul know that one cares. Like a simple *please* and *thank-you*. It costs nothing.

If only she considered bringing a gun to a gun fight. I'd stand by her side and take on my many menaces. We could be Butch Cassidy and the Sundance Kid. Maybe Bonnie and Clyde.

I shall remain grateful.

Joey's pal, Vince called him.

'Hey man. You wanna job? Good money. Be good for it.'

'Oh! I wish, man. I am a mess.'

'I want you to come to a presentation I am putting on. If you like what you see, I will let you in on the game. I will hold your hand through it all. I will mentor you, bro.'

ACN was a network marketing company set-up in the States in the early noughties. They offered large discounts to those signed up within the pyramid on a plethora of household services; phone, internet, television, power, hydro... You sign up, and you save. Good money. The more people signed up below you, the larger the discounts.

There were large conventions to attend and smaller household pitches set up with friends. A latter-day Avon lady or Tupperware party. A latter-day Ann Summers without the battery-operated fun and for the sterilized twenty-first century. The prospect of either the large convention or the intimate home gathering filled Joey with dread, but Vince was by nature a smooth-talker and a good friend who offered Joey the wisdom and support to do it. Joey recognized there could be a seriously good upside.

He struggled with Vince's bitten fingernails and thumbs but regretted deeply the whole exercise when their mutual pal, Devon came to his house for a presentation. Who doesn't want to shave off twenty-five per cent off what they gave to the abysmal cable companies? That bit was an easy sell.

But when Devon sat at Joey's family dining table and began – with no rhyme nor reason – to bleed from his forehead in the style of a statue of the Virgin Mary, that vision, that spectre weeping scarlet tear drops, he could take no more. The god that had thrown him a bone was now having an unabated belly laugh at him.

I swear this is the meanest stunt yet, he thought.

Devon saw them staring aghast at him, touched his head when he felt the tiniest trickle and he ran to the bathroom, but Joey just had to get him out of the house, knowing full well that the washroom would then be off limits for him for years. This is the only place in the world he could urinate.

'You have to leave. Please leave. You do not understand. You must go.'

'Joey, he is fine. Relax. He is about to…. *sign!*'

'No, Vince. Devon OUT!'

KA-BOOOOOOOOOOOOOOOM!

As the car sped off from his driveway, Joey cared not about having upset Vince, missed the deal nor having offended Devon. He was already on the hunt in the drawers to find the largest pair of scissors the family owned. He did not consider whether it was judicious or wise to slice his way through Mary's favourite tablecloth where Devon had squeezed vermillion from his forehead. It was a vintage piece of cloth that covered gracefully the lengthy table that seated ten at a canter. Or once covered it. No more. Now sliced by a twitching and well-meaning demented sort.

'This is the straw that breaks the camel's back, Silvio,' he heard her yell.

'I cannot take it anymore.'

Her fury hurt like hell, and this is what pushed him to try the personal development courses of the motivational speaker, Jim Rohn. He had to show he was trying something. His contrition was clear.

> "Don't wish it were easier, wish you were better. Don't wish for fewer problems, wish for more skills. Don't wish for less challenge, wish for more wisdom."

That was one of his.

> "Days are expensive. When you spend a day, you have one less day to spend. So make sure you **spend each one wisely**."

This too. Jim knew. Jim seemed to have the answers. Joey was hooked.

> "**Don't** join an easy crowd, for you won't grow. Go where the expectations and the demands to perform are high."

And it was through Rohn that Joey was introduced to Rhonda Byrne's *The Secret*. Joey put up his vision board at his home. This was the key to manifestation. Picture one's goals and they will come.

Mine shall be a family room in a downtown house, with a clear view of the CN Tower, a smiling man and my grandparents as a guide to keep me alive. Nonno, Nonna. Look at me. I am doing this to show you, you were right to love me and to believe in me. I am moving up fast in the company. I am going to do it. It is so hard. I cannot leave the house some days. I cannot stand the conventions, and the house parties make me want to barf. Every second of every day, I want to run.

But I am staying as strong as can be. Vince is taking me to North Carolina for a convention. I left a pitch in Muskoka last week. How on earth will I make it in an aeroplane to the United States?

Nonna, I still think of joining you early before my time. But I know this will not please you, and there are billions of years for us to hold hands when the time is right. I need to push forward. Tira avanti. God, I miss you so much. I wish I had kissed you, Nonno. I wish I had held you to the end, Nonna. I am so sorry. I love you.

'Va tutto bene, Govi. Essere buono. Rendi orgogliosa tua madre. Questo è il tuo lavoro adesso. Il mio cavaliere è qui. Sto bene.'

'It is all right, Govi. Be good. Make your mother proud. This is your job now. My horseman is here. I am fine.'

It was September 16th, 2011 when the phone rang in the middle of the night. Joey answered it, Mary rushed to the phone. He handed it to her and looked over her shoulder and nodded sagely to his father, mouthing the words, 'It is a boy.'

They went to the hospital, for Joey just a big building full of blood. He had discarded most of his nice clothes and turned up in some unreasonably uncool *melange*. But it did not matter. Luke was born. The child would never know how he helped to meld this family together at a moment when they might have fallen away, splintered by the suicide of Joey Tomaselli. They were not out of the woods yet. Not by a long chalk.

That spot next to Nonna shall remain unoccupied. For now.

Chapter 16

His odd behaviour showed no signs of abating.

'Where is the Water Bandit?' a pal would ask in his now-extended absence.

They all knew where he was. They chuckled, but it was with love and in no way mean-spirited.

Joey was in the washroom.

Oh, I wish someone would come in.

One of them would rescue him soon.

He couldn't touch the door handle. Also, the faucets were on full, for if he turned one off, he would only need to wash his hands again. It was one of those perennial and eternal puzzles. Schrödinger's cat. Does a fridge light turn off when it is closed? If a tree falls in a forest and it doesn't make a sound, is Joey still wrong? And crazy?

Lord knows the level of psychosis were there to be any splash-back from the urinal. (At least, he could now go away from his parents' bathroom.)

If he had to shake hands, he would consider that right arm as good as amputated for days. He would become left-handed.

He was dating a beautiful older lady, perhaps ten years his senior. She could have had anyone, but last weekend, there she was, nestled into a luxury hotel next to Niagara Falls, concerned for and caring for

Joey Tomaselli. She watched him sandblast himself in the shower for hours, as she gave him a motherly pep-talk. He remembered how she had woken up to him pacing up and down in pain, like a caged beast. He tried to verbalize the pain, as they lay in bed, but this was not easy.

The Water Bandit had given himself his own title, self-imposed, self-nominated, self-ordained. He was the President of the United States of Hypochondria. And now visited a walk-in clinic, where one did not need an appointment, thirty times in three months. That was one visit every three days. There was only one doctor on duty there, so they became well-acquainted.

Joey spent much of that winter waiting either in the car park of the walk-in or in the waiting rooms inside. The doctor was a kind and patient lady, who finally had the inspired idea to suggest that he call the Centre for Addiction and Mental Health (CAMH) in downtown Toronto. She had heard the broadest spectrum of symptoms and was able to now deduce that a specialist in the field of mental health was required.

CAMH enjoyed and enjoys a global reputation and is observed, visited, and heralded by mental health experts from around the world as a pioneer in techniques and in the vanguard of success rates, fixing the sick. The doctor gave Joey a number, no specific target, and no referral. Just call them. It would be good for him to have this as an exercise. She trusted him to comply.

Here Joey would meet professional number SIXTEEN. Is it wise to stick or twist on sixteen? Depends which cards have been shown. If you happen to be dealt a soft 16 (like Ace-5), you should never surrender and you should never stand. Your first option is to double but only if the dealer shows a weak 4, 5, or 6. If not, then hit.

Go for it, Joey. Twist.

When the doctor walked in, Joey was in the swivel chair in the middle of the office. His hands and his feet were in the air. This was the doctor's first impression, and first impressions cannot hurt if one is being authentic. Tell the truth. Be yourself. If one pretends to be someone else, one will end up with the wrong job, partner, friends.

Always be yourself. It is the fast track to a perfect world. Cut through the nonsense.

'Hello, Joey.'

Joey launched into his story. This story. He was perhaps ten minutes in when the white coat had heard enough.

'OK, I hear you. Phobia, you say. I think I know what you need. It is a drug called *Cipralex.*'

'I would rather die,' Joey said without a hint of meanness. He was never mean, even in his zeniths of frustration. He did rise to leave but was stopped momentarily.

'But wait, before you go. I do know two guys who may be able to help you.'

'One is out of town right now. He is a former boss of this place. He is now a prof at the University of Toronto with a private practise.'

'And the other?'

'He is fantastic. Doctor Newman. I think he is perfect for you.'

'Let's do it. If he is here now, let's do it.'

Cognitive behavioral therapy (CBT) is a psycho-social intervention that aims to improve mental health. CBT focuses on challenging and changing unhelpful cognitive distortions (e.g. thoughts, beliefs, and attitudes) and behaviors, improving emotional regulation and the development of personal coping strategies that target solving current problems. Originally, it was designed to treat depression, but its uses have been expanded to include treatment of a number of mental health conditions, including anxiety. CBT includes a number of cognitive or behavior psychotherapies that treat defined psychopathologies using evidence-based techniques and strategies.

CBT is based on the combination of the basic principles from behavioral and cognitive psychology. It is different from historical approaches to psychotherapy, such as the psychoanalytic approach where the therapist looks for the unconscious meaning behind the behaviors and then formulates a diagnosis. Instead, CBT is a "problem-focused" and "action-oriented" form of therapy, meaning it is used to treat specific problems related to a diagnosed mental disorder. The therapist's role is to assist the client in finding and practicing effective strategies to address the identified goals and decrease symptoms of the disorder. CBT is based on the belief that thought distortions and maladaptive behaviors play a role in the development and maintenance of psychological disorders and that symptoms and associated distress can be reduced by teaching new information-processing skills and coping mechanisms.

—Wikipedia

He met Doctor Newman three days later. He was an older gent, clipped hair, spectacles, a disarming smile, gentle tone, searching grey eyes.

'I have to say, Joey, I am not cheap. It is two hundred and fifty per session. But the good news is that after eight hours, you will be equipped to move on. I promise.'

Doc leaned in, smiled and nodded over his glasses, a confident glint in his eyes.

'Let's do it.'

One last roll of the dice. I am not even going to stick on seventeen. Pull an ace, Joey, if you have to.

They went straight into breathing exercises and Joey felt air released out of his over-inflated tyre of his mind immediately.

'Now I want you to come for a walk with me. And show me what bothers you. We are going to tackle a whole chunk of this together today.'

They stepped out into the hallways of the hospital and walked until there was a doorknob with a red mark on it.

'That there.'

'Touch it!'

'No way.'

'Touch it! Please. It cannot hurt you. I promise.'

'I can't.'

'Talk me through why. I am touching it. I am fine. I am more powerful than *it*.'

'I know, but...'

'Touch it. Make massive steps, make progress right here. In one minute from now, you can be powerful in this fight. I like you, Joey. I know you can beat this. You are the one really in control.'

Joey walked back into his office fifteen minutes later and sat down.

'You did really well. And now I want you to take a real leap of faith with me. Let's make today a RED-LETTER day – literal and metaphorical, one to remember for all time,' as the doctor sat down too and looked into his eyes on the same level as he.

'What is it?'

'I think you trust me, don't you?'

He nodded.

'Good, you are right to, I think what you've seen so far today shows you can trust me. You have done really well. But we are about to obliterate this phobia. Phobias are always irrational. Fears are rational. Not phobias.'

And with that, he took a pen and coloured a red dot on some blotting paper. He wrote the word, BLOOD above it in scarlet.

Joey pushed himself back in his chair. In horror.

'I am going to tell you a secret. When blood touches air, it becomes harmless and utterly unable to hurt us, especially the way you believe it can.'

'Is that true?'

'Yes.' They both spoke as if it were blood. It was ink. He had seen it come from the nib.

Three minutes of silence. It was the same silence Joey had been taught to use in closing a big deal.

'Now, touch THAT!

This is insane. But don't run, Joey. He is telling the truth. Look what he did in the hallway. You touched that. Now touch this. No ka-boom! You're still alive.

And that was that.

Within hours, he swaggered past red paint and no longer tip-toed, shoeless, like a weird and deviant clod past hot dog stands and their ketchup spatters.

'When you go home tonight, have half a beer with Silvio.'

'But I have not touched a drop in three years…'

'Good, but you are now in control. You have showed that you are not a slave to it. Now you are the boss.'

He did. And he was in control.

He even drank out of a bottle with a red label. The first sip was so hard with no safety net of meds. He expected the ground to move like it had that crazy night after his final spliff. But as with the doctor earlier that day, the red text and ink had not harmed him. And now the beer. Silvio smiled at him across the kitchen table and thought of the baby steps he had seen him take thirty years previously. He tried to think which gave him greater satisfaction.

With two sessions left, he told the doctor about the pending and looming trip to North Carolina for the convention.

'Oh good, we can do this. This is the perfect test.'

So, it proved to be. Tests are never meant to be easy. Surmountable and nearing impossible. But still surmountable.

The flight down was with Vince's cousin, Marco.

The positive mental imagery instilled - and the commensurate power granted - by Doctor Newman allowed for a smooth passage through the hard-stares and meanness of customs and immigrations and the harsh duration of the flight down there. But his spiritual gas ran out as soon as the wheels touched the tarmac on U.S. soil. The pain kicked in, an anguish that was now up to nine and a half.

He retrenched to the sanctuary of his hotel room and sought the calming words of Jim Rohn on his laptop. Jim Rohn could talk him down. Couldn't he?

Marco found him cowering in a corner and talked him into walking to the convention centre. Twenty thousand others be damned. Let's do it.

Soon he was again found, this time crying near registration.

A sweet lady asked what was wrong, and when he blubbered out some words that partially connected the dots of his horror, she generously pointed out that it was a miracle that he was there at all. He should extract much strength, courage, and pride from this.

But the rest of the three days, he was perpetually on the point of similar breakdowns, similar nadirs of terror.

Yes, he had posted pictures on Facebook of him posing happily and proudly with his pals, but inside he was in utter turmoil, viscerally and mentally destroyed. Sandra had called to congratulate him on doing what he was doing, but he knew it to be a lie. He kept her on the line, left the building and wept and sobbed openly down the phone to her, trying to explain the extent of the cutting and perpetual pain.

If only I could call Doctor Newman... he thought,

but the conditions were that he was on his own.

They would discuss is all upon his return. No safety net.

As the flight home approached, the pain subsided, but this time, the physical journey at thirty-five thousand feet sent him into a tail-spin. The cousins were on different flights.

Suck it up, Joey.

A passenger complained about his pacing about, up and down, up and down, up and down. Several gave him concerned glances askance.

The stewardess was fortunately an understanding type. She allowed him to stay in the bathroom for landing, completely against all regulations. But better in there, than sweating and twitching and yelling in public. He splashed his face all the way to the terminal.

He went out that night and drank vodka – not many - in downtown Toronto. He now felt powerful in his *mano-a-mano* with booze. He now knew when to quit. He had one more session with Doctor Newman. This man was changing his life. Even removing one evil from his list of horrors was adequate for him to know he was going to push forward. *Tira avanti.*

The last time they met, Doctor Newman again came in close, and looked deeply into Joey's eyes. He said, 'You're a funny guy. You're hilarious. I really like you. And listen to me now. You deserve to get better, but there is NOTHING wrong with you mentally. Well, you have your quirks, of course,' and they both laughed.

'What I should say is that the reason you aren't right is that there is a physical problem. I don't think anything thing is mentally wrong with you I feel something is *physically* wrong with you.

He recalled his Las Vegas mirage, he remembered believing there was something up that concurred with Doctor Newman.

'Your phobia has gone, and your OCD is down to a trickle of what it was. Now you need to use this to search for the answer. You have made giant steps. I won't give you a prescription for any meds, I have no referral for you, and I do not know where you go from here. I know you have knocked two massive burdens off your back. You flew to the United States, Joey. Use all of this as a mast, not an anchor.'

Farewell, my friend. Hippocrates would be proud of you. You spilled blood for me. I am forever grateful.

Bocca al lupo, Joey Tomaselli!

It was true, he was down to one shower a day, he could touch things. He had seen whom he believed to be the best therapist in the world, and this filled his sails.

He took a recruitment job in the grim mid-winter of 2012/2013. It was commission-only, the drive was hell, and the paydays were depressingly meagre. And it was while he was there one day, questioning the wisdom of his being there, when his friend, Sandra called.

'I know you're sick of friends suggesting doctors, but I want you to please try this amazing woman. Imagine if you had refused to see Doctor Newman.'

'Will she touch me?'

'Not necessarily. She is called Ingrid. She practises *reiki.*'

'Oh god, what is that?'

'Japanese. She heals through her hands. Energy. She helped me. And some of my friends. Not one was disappointed.'

'Will she touch my head?'

'Not if you don't want it.'

And the next day, he pulled up outside her house in the suburb of Scarborough. He went into her basement, beneath the house where she lived with her son. She was a kind and thoughtful lady, who let Joey speak, and she was clearly engaged and invested.

She told him of a strong female presence in Joey's life which he took to be Nonna. She also told him that he would soon travel, move out of his current address, and receive forgiveness from his ex-.

The *reiki* itself felt really good. And then he mistakenly thought she was going to touch his head...

Ka-boooooom! *KA-BOOOOOOOOOOM! KA-BOOOO OOOOOOOOM!*

And there he was again. A shell, glass-eyed, shaking. Doomed. No more! No more!

One step forward, five steps back.

May 2012

And then ***that old man*** came again when Joey remained in that deep trench, unable to move for fear of shrapnel and torture and imminent death. That reluctant and benevolent and true leader. When he had come the last time with the words, 'I don't like seeing you like this, buddy,' Joey thought it to be a one-off. But it was not a one-off. He was back, and now, and only because it was his father, that Joey listened.

'I know someone at Sunnybrook,' said Silvio. 'Let's give it a try?'

Joey gave in. Silvio had funded much of his search for salvation, just as he had that trip to Italy long, long ago to set his boy up for soccer glory in the homeland. Joey knew he had to go along. Our Glory Boy was aiming for a last-minute winner from outside the box.

The biggest fight of his life, where his very existence was at best a toss-up, was still to come.

Well, two fights. One to get perhaps well. The other just to stay alive, as deep and dark thoughts of suicide returned. Perhaps the Glory Boy will ignominiously put the ball into Row Z behind the goal to the groans of the watching hordes...

17

TWIST ON 19

The journey is almost over. Who will put this poor boy out of his misery?

As overtures were made to Sunnybrook, there was another angle of hope in the shape of a caring Chinese doctor by the name of Xiu. Joey's dear friend from ACN, Angela and her aunt, Sandra (so reminiscent of Nonna) had recommended him. He loved them so much that he went along with her suggestion, but now he was done. Or he was until he met Doctor Xiu, who embodied that Hippocratic Oath to its fully intended extent. He was calm, tender, caring, patient, truthful, understanding and utterly beautiful in his Zen spirit.

After hearing every single word of Joey's circuitous and meandering and undoubtfully tragic story, he sat back, touched the ends of his fingers together in a truly measured gesture, and spoke finally.

'Are you a betting man, Joey?'

'What do you mean?'

'I want to offer you a deal. I know the best neurosurgeon in the land. He is at Saint Michael's. If I can get you in to see him, and he says that you are fine, and just need *Cipralex,* will you do it, please?'

'I'll do anything in that case. I will take heroin if you say I am fine. I trust you to that degree,' Joey said.

'Well, it is now July the 16th. He has a long waiting list. Let's see what I can do. But you gave the right answer. Well done.'

They shook hands.

Thank you, Doctor Xiu. I love you.

Joey walked towards the door. He turned and still not tired of communicating with this saintly man, asked one last question.

'I have been asked to play in a soccer tournament in August. Am I ok to play? If I take it easy.'

'I think it best to miss it. I don't know why I am telling you this. But I think it best to miss it.'

I am on nineteen. And I am going to twist.

What kind of lunatic or utterly informed card-counting genius would do THAT? My money is on lunatic. Or it would be, but I know I am NOT CRAZY.

18

Chapter

TWIST ON TWENTY?

September 2012

oey started as a recruitment consultant the day he opened his mail from St Michael's hospital. He had an appointment with Dr. Xiu's neurosurgeon, Doctor Harold Gerschwin on December the 2nd. Still three months away. But it was something.

The job was closer to home, far nicer and with a salary. He was shifting labor around industrial sites for a vast enterprise. He even made decent pals with a lovely co-worker called Bruno. That first day they bonded over a *You Tube* clip of the comedian, Sebastian Maniscola. His skit, *What's Wrong with People?* made Joey laugh in a manner that he had forgotten he could muster. The long-forgotten art of mirth, and what magic she brings. The release of endorphins trapped for three years rushed his mind and then his physical being. He relaxed and felt mild euphoria, and key to this joy – as much as the comedic clip - was the potential unravelling of his case with Doctor Gerschwin, the best in the business Doctor Xiu had called him. He also knew not to get too carried away.

He was also looking forward to getting away on the long weekend with his pals, Savi and Marcelo Repole. Savi and Marcelo were uncle and nephew but given the prodigious and lengthy coupling years of the Italian male and female, they were from a large family and were close in age, close enough to be brothers. They were great company, and a warm Saturday and Sunday at a pristine lake beckoned. However, one might have seriously wondered whether it was a wise move to go tubing on the back of a rapid speedboat, especially given Doctor Newman's assertion that there was something physically wrong with Joey and that Doctor Xiu had – albeit somewhat viscerally – advised that he not go play soccer.

The others were unaware of the fragility of Joey's frame. He himself appeared blasé about any risk. He had after all conquered some malevolent demons of late. On the third or fourth steep-banked turn, Joey flew from the inflatable and hit the water at a velocity perilous to a healthy person. He went under, came up, gulped for air and heard a familiar noise on his eardrum.

Ka-booom! Ka-boooooooom! Ka-booooooooooooom!

It took all his might to swim to the boat, where he was helped in before being dropped at the dock at his request. Savi then took some pics of them, his camera set up on auto and on a small tripod.

When they see my face in the future, they will see how close to death I am, he thought.

He felt his face to be a mask. He tried to smile but was sure it looked like a grimace and close to tears.

When I am gone, they will know from these photographs. Then every-thing will become clear to them. They will know. They will know I was being serious. It will be too late. I am hurting again.

December 2nd, 2012

Joey drove to St. Michael's hospital on a brisk inside-of-a-walk-in-refrigerator morning.

He met Doctor Harold Gerschwin, the last such meeting – with a new medical expert - in Joey's short life. No more.

Basta! Enough!

Gerschwin was perhaps forty-five, a pleasant disposition that belied the economy of words required by such a busy man. His waiting list was eighteen months, but Doctor Xiu had shoved him audaciously - and yet with Zen - to the front of the line.

Lovely human being.

Joey told his full story about as rapidly as he could. He sensed this doctor was busier than the others and so delivered as concise a version as possible.

'Good, well we need an MRI.'

'I have had one already. Three years ago. November sixteenth, 2009.'

Joey pulled a CD from his jacket pocket.

'You've had this for three years?' the doctor shuffled back in his seat as if to expect a surprise. His eyes widened when he observed the images on the disc.

'I see. I see. OK, I need just one really quick X-ray and then we will see where that takes us.'

He seemed to be aware of where this might lead him, but like any good detective, - be it Poirot, Holmes or Marple - needed iron-clad proof to confirm his suspicion. One would not want to look silly or shoddy.

'Come with me, please, Joey.'

The doctor was careful to open all doors *en route*. Joey felt as if he were a special cargo. There was both a visceral comfort and a gut-feeling concern attached to this. And he was minutes away from finding out why. But we have already heard about the Confidence of Ignorance. Sometimes not knowing is better, Sometimes, knowledge is a truly scary and wholly destructive state, capable of hollowing out the strongest soul, never mind one who had lived a daily hell for nigh-on three revolutions of the sun. They entered the X-ray room.

'Stand there. Please keep your left shoulder to the wall. And look up to the ceiling, please, Joey.'

'Easy, Doctor.'

It lasted several seconds, and then he was asked to follow the doctor back to his office, again all doors were held open and they moved slowly and purposefully.

'Take a seat back here, please. I will be back in ten minutes.'

'Thanks, Doctor.'

He looked at the clock. It was twenty-four minutes past the hour. Nine minutes later, Dr. Gerschwin returned.

This is a man who knows about the Oath, he thought.

'I don't know how to tell you this, Joey...'

Ka-boom!

Just one ka-boom!

'...but you've been walking around with your head and neck hanging by a string for three years. It is somewhat of a miracle that you are alive. You have a torn ligament in your C1 vertebrae.'

'*Shit! There is something wrong with me! he thought. I knew it.*

And he considered that Nevada desert mirage. Fresh water from an oasis was there, it was clear. But the danger was not gone. This was just information. This was knowledge, but so is expecting an air-raid or waiting for a hurricane in a beach shack. *The Confidence of Ignorance.*

And now came the mixed emotions.

'What does this mean, please, Doctor?'

'You need *major* surgery.'

He checked his calendar.

'I can get you in on February thirteenth.'

He made intense eye contact.

'I need to tell you something. There is a fifty-fifty chance that you either survive or you can die or be paralyzed.'

'Can I avoid this surgery?'

'Joey, if you slip outside today or take a ten kilometre per hour fender-bender on the way home, you WILL die.'

That's why he opened all the doors for me. Jesus.

'It is either one hundred per cent pain or suicide versus a toss of a coin? Let's do it, Doctor. And thank you.'

His trust was total.

'Good. You could just die in your sleep if you turn the wrong way. This is truly serious. We will do what we call C1 fusion surgery.

212

Maybe ten screws, three or four plates and a rod to fuse your verte-brae. I can fix you. You will lose 1.5 millimetres of your range of mo-tion and contact sports and weights over fifty pounds are out. For life.'

Who on earth twists on twenty? **This** *guy, Joey Tomaselli. I think there is an ace at the top of the deck. He walks and talks like an ace. Doctor Xiu may have fixed the pack. Shuffled my ace to the top.*

He left the office, and was immersed in sadness, anger, fear, joy, and confusion.

He thought about the times he might have snapped his neck. The boat ride, the car crash, even the sex.

He drove home with his hazard lights on and at a snail's pace. In the three-quarter blind spirit of the ninety-year-old lass, sitting on a cushion and with spectacles so thick as to resemble the bottom of a jam jar, trundling along in the outside lane, his sloth might have created more of a peril than speeding at 150 kmh.

There were many yells of 'Asshole' and 'Screw you, buddy.' He did not respond. To move a muscle might be the end of him.

The *doppelgaenger* twin of the miracle of his having survived to date allowed for him to pull the jeep onto Silvio's driveway. In one piece.

His old man was eating at the head of the long dining table. Mary sat by him, tired, but still in obvious adoration and her own version of robust obeisance.

'Everything OK? Are we done yet?' he said with a gentle mocking and loving smile.

'I have something to tell you both.

He sat down.

They were both aghast as Joey recounted the verdict of Doctor Harold Gerschwin and the upcoming plan. Dad went from smile to stony face. Mom's face was impossible to read, perhaps in shock. Blank. Hard to know. *Heads or tails.*

Tick tock. Tick tock. Intermittently entwined with a polite-ish *ka-boom!*

✷

February 12, 2013.

T minus one day.

I cannot sleep. I could be dead tomorrow. In a chair for life. That won't last long, I swear. You can do this, Joey. Channel the vision of Doctor Newman. Channel the wisdom of Doctor Xiu. Channel the neat skill of Doctor Gerschwin. You are in good hands. But you still might die. Or plan to slit your wrists in a wheelchair. All options are in play. You twisted on twenty. Jesus, man. Only an ace can save me. I can pull an ace, Hit me! Ace, ace, ace.

They drove to the hospital as a family. Joey did not sleep, but told himself he would have a full day of sleep, so what's the difference?

Mary carried a prayer book from St. Michael that her neighbour, Mrs. Conti had given her the previous year. He had read it every day. Now they were going to St. Mike's hospital. It seemed fitting, if not somewhat portentous and encouragingly profound. She gave it to her only son. He also held the pamphlets from Nonno's and Nonna's funerals.

There were a couple of dozen people in the check-in area to the hospital. He was in the same area as those just going off for a consultation. He was going in for life-or-death surgery, - *how could this be?* - and this cranked up his anxiety. He could not sit down. There would be plenty of time for that if he were in a chair. Until he could access a razor blade, that is. The emotions were coming in waves now, but also building to a crescendo. He stood expressionless until the dam broke. The sobs began and would not abate. He recalled strange looks and worried countenances. Mary and Silvio stood by in solidarity.

Poor Mom. Poor Dad. I really put you through it, don't I? But I cannot breathe now. Ka-Boooooom!

Other than being asked to let go of the pamphlets...

Blank.

The next thing he knew he was in a gown and shower cap being wheeled into a very cold room.

'Hey, Doctor. Did you have a drink last night?'

'Don't worry, Joey. I am fine.'

'Did you fight with your wife? When are you at your best? First, second or third operation of the day?'

Joey was on his stomach. Had he taken his last ever step?

'You are number two today. You'll be fine. I want you to count down from ten when the nurse puts this needle into the back of your hand.'

Did you properly say your goodbyes, Joey? No, I didn't. Mom! Dad! MOM!!!! Ten…Nine…. Eight… Seeeevvvvvveeeennnnnn…..

Buona note… Ciao.

He would remain ignorant of the discussion the doctor had with Silvio and Mary in the hallways when they were told that Joey had lost his vital signs. Ah the Confidence of Ignorance. He was now dead on the table.

PART FIVE

Chapter 19

The message Joey had left us was not a suicide note. It was a YouTube video, well, a YouTube audio. He had called it *Tira Avanti*. Push Forward. It is over an hour long and was a brave and honest and yet measured and disciplined document. It is still there today. Were Mary to sit and listen to it, she would weep, remembering her only son. Nadia and Sandra too. And Silvio. Friends press play from time to time to be reminded of his voice, while strangers around the world have been directed to it in their search for comfort and inspiration in their own struggle against mental demons and the search for an answer to their unending and mean pain.

'When you don't look, you hurt people and that's not fair. WHEN YOU DO NOT LOOK, YOU HURT PEOPLE, AND THAT IS NOT FAIR'

The strangers know about Joey's benevolent message, because one night, in the depths of anguish, Joey posted on the *YouTube* comments of Doctor Daniel Amen's *Illumeably* video. The story of his nephew with a tumour and a cyst invading his brain, while he punched little girls and made suicide art. A nine-year-old. Within seconds, Joey's laptop had pinged. And again. Five likes, twenty likes. Love hearts. Sad face. Fifty likes. A hundred. The next morning eleven hundred and thirty likes.

'Please tell your *whole* story,' they urged and implored.

And so, he did.

And back here in the hospital, a poem read out at his grandfather's funeral now seemed so apt. It had been written by a heralded but troubled Welshman*, but its pointed relevance knows no international borders. It is a universal truth. Poetry is like that. And so is death.

> Do not go gentle into that good night,
> *Any* age should burn and rave at close of day;
> Rage, rage against the dying of the light.

He now heard no voices in the operating room. No beeps from the machines. In his new lifeless darkness, Joey saw a bright light. The brightest, and he felt the ecstatic comfort of knowing no pain. The confidence of ignorance. Euphoria and rapture.

*Walk to it. She is there for you. Does he hear **her** voice? Govi!*

> Good men, the last wave by, crying how bright
> Their frail deeds might have danced in a green bay,
> Rage, rage against the dying of the light.

Yes, it is her voice. But it contains an urgent message.

> And you, my *grandson*, there on the sad height,
> Curse, bless, me now with your fierce tears, I pray.

'*Non è il momento. Non ancora. Non è così che finisce, amore mio.*'
'*It is not time. Not yet. This is not how it ends, my love.*'

And rage, he did. With every ounce of his faded and now medically - but not spiritually - dead being.

He turned from the light and from the spectre of his beloved old lady. Govi walked back to life itself.

---

* *Dylan Thomas (1914-1953) Do not go gentle into that good night.*

Beep. Beep. Beep.
Beep. Beep. Beep.
Beep. Beep. Beep.
Beep. Beep. Beep.

✿

What should have been a four-hour surgery was – counterintui-
tively – shorter because of the extent of the tear. There was less ligament to cut, so badly was it damaged. But there was time for him to
have died and come back to life. He is a resurrection. He is her life.

He came around in a neck brace. Opened a single eye.

'I am thirsty,' he struggled to say.

There were two nurses there. One came to him with a Q-Tip
soaked in water for him to suck on.

'Am I paralyzed?'

The other picked up a pin, stuck it minimally in the ball of his
foot, and asked, 'Can you feel that?'

Pause.

Oh sweet, sweet pain.

This gave way to utter and unleashed agony in his neck The *ka-
boom* had shifted.

He pushed the buzzer every five minutes to pump himself with
morphine. He then embraced the pain, channeled it as an ally, for it
meant he could be cured. Possibly forever. Of course, there was still
the cruellest path to pass down – the one that, yes, fixed his neck,
but did not address the other problems. This was still an unknown.

In Newman, I trust. In Xiu, I trust. In Gerschwin, I trust.

A new mantra for a new époque.

The morphine was more-ish, but he soon announced,

'I won't get addicted. I can conquer those devils. As soon as I don't
need it, you can take it away.'

So much of the time, not even Sister Morphine could mask the
pain.

He had to sleep sitting up for three months. This too would be easy. Perhaps the toughest thing for him to deal with that day was the catheter.

'Who gave you permission to put that in?' he asked the nurse, clipping across the tiles.

'It is normal, required for any procedure as intense as yours.'

'Well can I have it out, please? And please find the oldest nurse in this building to do it for me, please.'

A boy has his pride, you know.

Its removal was as painful as the surgery. But now he was liberated. The three other men in the ward may have chuckled. Maybe not. For now, he slept. And still not out of the woods.

Two days later, he was allowed to go home. February the fifteenth, 2013.

The pain killers were useless against the pain. He considered going back to hospital.

It has been four years. Suck it up, Joey, he thought. You've beaten four players, left them for dead, littered across the field, rounded the goalkeeper, just don't spoon it over the crossbar now. You've done all the hard work. This is the easy part.

Think of Newman. Think of Xiu. Think of Gerschwin. The holy trinity. My holy trinity.

The neck brace was to stay on until May the first. He had a lazy-boy chair, in which to sleep and repose. Showers were hard, for he could not move his head. There were eighteen staples in the neck, covering a scar that would extend for five inches.

⚙

Some nights he met friends, who wanted to hear all the gruesome details. He went to a hockey game even and got used to the weird looks. He had got used to the weird looks for years, he chuckled to himself. He remembered the odd frowns and concerned miens of the old ladies in *Shoppers Drugmart* with their prunes and toilet paper. They would be proud of him. No longer worrying people in the grocery store.

He quit the painkillers early, as he had predicted and promised. This bookmarked a sturdy and robust determination.

You've got this, Joey. You are in control.

He heard Doctor Newman's voice at such times, and pictured Doctor Xiu's Zen quarter-smile.

They would still not know if there had been success until the next X-ray on May 1st with Doctor Gerschwin who now beckoned him in – in his mind's eye – as the bright light had on the operating table.

Many people think that the call for help given by pilots and ship's captains is 'May Day! May Day!' But it is not. It is the French, *'M'aidez! M'aidez!' Help me. Help me.* How apt that on this May day, this May the first, Joey Tomaselli no longer needed help.

'This looks beautiful,' Doctor Gerschwin purred. 'And you can leave that neck brace here. Go live your life, young man.'

Joey scanned the imaging on the doctor's wall.

'I look like an Ikea bed set before assembly.'

Gerschwin belly-laughed. Joey had not seen this before. Then another first from the inscrutable and understandably unemotional surgeon.

'I brought you a card, Doctor.'

He looked surprised. Taken aback. Joey had donated all the money he had to the hospital in Doctor Gerschwin's name. The receipt was there for five hundred and twenty-two dollars thirty-seven cents. Every penny. The card read,

'I want to thank you for saving my life. I cannot even start to explain my last four years of hell. I have seen nineteen professionals including two other neurologists before you. They all said I was either fine or crazy. Or that because I was fine, I was crazy. Thank you for seeing what they did not. What they could not. I know we do not know each other, but I love you, buddy.'

Whether it was the note itself, or the money or the utterly disarming and fraternal honesty in the last line, Doctor Gerschwin welled up and became glassy eyed from the unabashed gratitude and decency of Joey Tomaselli, the newly ordained poet.

He walked away with a swagger.

✿

His pal, Sandro soon arranged a job interview for a new mobile sales app called Sammy, whose offices were in the plush Soho Hotel downtown. He got the job. Things were happening in quick succession.

On June the first, his friend, Ralph who lived by the new office at The Soho, said to Joey, "Come live with me."

Silvio and Mary were somewhat dubious when Joey announced this to them later that day. They had witnessed many well-meaning false dawns. But Joey packed, and as Ingrid said he would, he left. And even more intriguing was that he could see the CN Tower. The first night was a hell of a challenge. He woke up in shock, but he channelled his holy trinity of white coats. Newman, Xiu, Gerschwin. And it worked. Of course, it did.

He could even see the forty-fifth floor of Niels' building where the horror had happened on April the sixteenth all those years ago.

I have come full circle – kind of -, but with a nudge into a parallel universe where I actually do this. Succeed.

This wonderfully bizarre outer body experience flooded him with euphoria.

But tests lay ahead. Ralph set obstacles for him to overcome, in the spirit of Doctor Newman's urging him to touch scarlet and rouge. Mary was no longer there to clean up after him Hansel and Gretel style. So, when he left the sink faucets on for ten hours, Ralph took a deep breath and decided to brawl – spiritually - with the OCD beast. He forced Joey to walk without slippers, and even had their shower soaps touch, squished together in a maelstrom of contact and shared molecules.

'Joey, you'll be fine,' were the same words with the same intonation, cadence and love that Doctor Newman had uttered. And again, it was correct and truthful.

'You either clean or you go home,' Ralph said in the next ultimatum. And Joey cleaned.

And then Ralph knew it was time. Like releasing a mended bird into the wild, he then said the kind words.

'You have until September the first to find your own place.'

It is time.

Joey was eating lunch with his pal from work, Ryan whose mother had joined them. The subject turned to where Joey was going to live.

'I am a real estate agent. Leave it to me,' she said.

In another step on a path of least resistance that was all working to Joey's benefit, he relented and said, 'Sure.'

The townhouse he saw that afternoon had just gone on the market that day. It was an end unit with three floors and a roof terrace on Strachan and East Liberty, a four-minute walk from Lake Ontario and a magnificent vista of downtown, also minutes away on foot. It was on the land of the original Toronto settlement of Old York. Beautiful old warehouses and the perverse romance of an eighteenth-century jailhouse now mixed with high rises and restaurants, supermarkets, banks and pet stores.

'This is the place,' he said. 'How much is it?'

'560 is the asking price. You need to offer that today. I can get it for you if so. Twenty couples have already been here.'

'Put in the offer,' he said. And he drove home to tell his parents.

Silvio responded with a doubting tone. 'Downtown? You tried *that* already. You can get a detached house near here for that kind of money.'

Joey got the call. Joey had the house.

And just because life can be beautiful, Silvio loved it.

Joey's old vision board was now complete. There was just one element to slot in. The Vegas mirage now came into focus. He had found his watering hole. It was no oasis. He was saved.

And it was time to go there – Las Vegas – for real.

He was late for the flight. It was a good thing. It left no time for piffling anxieties.

He was with A.J. and was meeting the others there.

When they landed, he exclaimed, 'Jesus. Sweet Jesus. I am here. And I am ok.'

'Let's go eat dinner, buddy,' said A.J. and they picked a nice restaurant.

When the friends were gathered and the food arrived, it was then he wept. For thirty minutes. Joy. Ecstasy. Rapture. Euphoria. Exultation. Elation. Bliss. No safety net, no pills, no pain., no sweats, shakes or horrors. His ear drums beat no more. Just the soft sound of laughter. He now noticed the small things, the artwork, the sounds, the faces, the sensations of life. Nothing sensational. Just sensations, the simple things. In Latin, *sentire*.

He breathed it in, and he felt each atom in his being fill up to the brim with the marvels… of life. Like one of those pyramids of martini glasses as the clear liquid falls from the top to the bottom, filling each *en route* like a true work of art.

And then what happened in Vegas, well, you know the rest…

Epilogue

J oey Tomaselli sits in his new house. *Sorry*, his new *home*. He stares at the CN Tower. It is lit up tonight. And rightly so. Next to it sits a harvest moon of rampant luminescence. It too lights the modern city.

He smiles and touches the tattoo on his left forearm. It is a tattoo of Saint Michael. Two old ladies walk the path between him and the tower. One seems to carry an arm of provisions. He seems to recognize them from a previous, nebulous and foggy life. Do they look to his balcony and smile? Old ladies are great like that. They understand the ways of the universe like we never could.

Miles away, Silvio and Mary are together, and happy. His sisters speak proudly over dinner of their brother. They and their friends sip wine, the pals listen intently and tingle with vicarious pride. Luke does not know how he saved them all. He might soon.

More distantly, a horseman and his bride walk on a southern European hillside, followed by a snorting stallion who obeys his master and eyes him with respect. For he sees a natural love between the two before him. The stars are again out, and they are the same ones that the young and now liberated man in the New World can see. The rich scents of the bakery pervade the pre-dawn air and on fine rafts. They reach the town square, which is lit by the fullest moon.

Each street corner holds a thousand memories of days gone - and yet to relish. They are young again. They have their lives to live.

And that young man thinks,

Who would twist on twenty? Who on this sweet earth would twist on twenty?

Not a crazy person. Not. A. Crazy. Person.

THE END

Acknowledgements

From Ian Thornton

I acknowledge the monumental courage and inspiring tenacity of Joey Tomaselli. The thousands of words herein are the truest testament to him. Joey, it was a pleasure working with you. And an honour. I look forward to my family and your family meeting one day under bluer skies. *Bravissimo*, my friend.

From Joey Tomaselli

I would like to extend a special thank-you to my dear family. My father, Silvio, my mother, Mary, Sandra, Nadia, Nick, Cassy and Luke. You have always been there for me and have given me all the love I needed to overcome my traumas.

I also want to thank Tari for bringing my story of mental awareness and stigma to life and adding an amazing author in Ian Thornton, who I thoroughly enjoyed working with.

I want this story to be told for ONE reason and one reason only. To edify others about my continued battles with my mental health and the reproach that comes with it.

Keep pushing forward. Salvation and redemption CAN be found. Never give up. Please

About the Author

Ian Thornton read Business Studies and German at Sheffield University between 1986 and 1989, where he earned a First-Class B.A. (Hons).

He has lived in many places including California, Costa Rica, Australia, Mexico, London, and his native and beloved Yorkshire before moving to Toronto in 2009.

In the 90s, Ian worked for Broadcast, TV World and Variety magazines. He is a co-founder of the global television industry publisher and market-leader, C21 Media.

His first novel, *The Great and Calamitous Tale of Johan Thoms* was published by Simon & Schuster in Canada in 2013, and, a year later, by HarperCollins in the U.K., U.S., and the Commonwealth. It was translated across Europe, taught at the Sorbonne, and received a Kirkus Star. https://www.ian-thornton.com/johan-thoms

Ian covered the Royal wedding in London for CTV, Canada's premier independent broadcaster, and has written for *Wisden Cricketer*, *The Guardian*, *The Hindu* and the Soho House magazine, *House*. He also wrote on the football World Cup in South Africa for the Canadian sports channel, *The Score*, and has worked for Queen's University in Ontario, where his team's project was presented at the White House as part of President Obama's new media initiative.

Ian is the official biographer of the Compton cricket club in California and has been a judge on the largest Latin American film festival, *Expresion en Corto*. He also edited and wrote for the leading San Miguel de Allende tourist guide and website, *Portal San Miguel*.

His second novel, *The Deaths and Afterlife of Aleister Crowley* was published to a fanfare in late 2019.

His third book, *My Year of Living Anonymously* is near completion, and an accompanying documentary feature will have its broadcast premiere on TVO in Canada in May 2021 and a theatrical premiere at the Hot Docs Film Festival. The scripted drama version of Ian's astonishing true-life story of his remarkable and accidental friendship with the world's most notorious hacker is next.

Ian lives in Toronto with his wife, Heather Gordon, and their two children, Laszlo and Clementine.

For more, please see www.ian-thornton.com

CPSIA information can be obtained
at www.ICGtesting.com
Printed in the USA
BVHW072052180421
605197BV00024B/210